Reporting China on the Rise

'As China struggles to enhance its "soft power" commensurate with the perceived world-power status, what is the role of foreign correspondents and what are the prisms through which they narrate their China tales in an ensemble? This volume provides a riveting account of the lifeworld of foreign correspondents in China and contributes importantly to the comparative dimension of media and journalists.'

Chin-Chuan Lee, Yu Shan Chair Professor of
Communication, National Chengchi University, Taiwan

Drawing on the structural-constructivist framework of *journalistic field* and habitus, *Reporting China on the Rise* examines the internal and external dynamics which are shaping the work of foreign correspondents in China during Xi Jinping's tenure.

This study presents findings from extensive surveys and interviews with current and former correspondents based in China. It aims to explore how they have responded, and continue to respond, to pressures from within the journalistic field (such as a transforming media industry), as well as from constant shifts in global geopolitics, and China's increasingly restrictive journalistic environment. These factors are shown to work together to relationally define the news production practice of these correspondents and, ultimately, shape the final news product.

Journalism in modern China has become a widely discussed, yet gravely under-researched topic, both for policy-makers and academics. *Reporting China on the Rise* seeks to open up discussions around the role of the foreign press in generating meaningful media coverage of this growing superpower. It will be an invaluable resource for students and researchers of Journalism and Media Studies.

Yuan Zeng is a lecturer in Media and Communication at the University of Leeds, UK, where she researches and teaches journalism studies. Her research focuses on the dynamics between international journalism and foreign policy, media, and social change in China and beyond. She has a PhD in media studies from City University of Hong Kong.

Routledge Focus on Communication and Society
Series Editor: James Curran

Routledge Focus on Communication and Society offers both established and early-career academics the flexibility to publish cutting-edge analyses on topical issues, research on new media or in-depth case studies within the broad field of media, communication and cultural studies. Its main concerns are whether the media empower or fail to empower popular forces in society; media organisations and public policy; and the political and social consequences of the media.

Bad News from Venezuela
Alan MacLeod

Reporting China on the Rise
Habitus and Prisms of China Correspondents
Yuan Zeng

Reporting China on the Rise

Habitus and Prisms of China
Correspondents

Yuan Zeng

Routledge
Taylor & Francis Group

LONDON AND NEW YORK

First published 2019 by Routledge

2 Park Square, Milton Park, Abingdon, Oxon OX14 4RN
605 Third Avenue, New York, NY 10017

Routledge is an imprint of the Taylor & Francis Group, an informa business

First issued in paperback 2022

Copyright © 2019 Yuan Zeng

Publisher's Note

The publisher has gone to great lengths to ensure the quality of this reprint but points out that some imperfections in the original copies may be apparent.

British Library Cataloguing-in-Publication Data
A catalogue record for this book is available from the British Library

Library of Congress Cataloging-in-Publication Data
A catalog record for this book has been requested

ISBN: 978-1-138-58641-3 (hbk)
ISBN: 978-1-03-233844-6 (pbk)
DOI: 10.4324/9780429504594

Typeset in Times New Roman
by Apex CoVantage, LLC

Contents

Illustrations

Figures

Tables

Acknowledgements

The birth of this book has been a painstaking yet fascinating journey.

I had developed an acute interest in foreign reporting since high school, hoping to become a foreign correspondent someday. Later on, however, I became increasingly doubtful about the prospect of a journalist's career, given China's tightened control of press and ideology. I have thus turned to teach and research as a choice. When I started my PhD studies at City University of Hong Kong in 2013, Xi Jinping upon taking office was already showing a strong-man governance style. China's rise to the world stage must have given him outsized confidence needed to revert the country back to echoes of hard authoritarianism. I decided, for my PhD dissertation, to investigate the milieus and prisms of foreign correspondents who try to make sense of a China on the rise.

This choice soon proved to be more challenging than I had expected. China was hypersensitive to any academic activities related to media studies, while foreign journalists were equally wary of being put under the radar of state surveillance if they dared to play a part in 'academic research.' Not only did relevant government bodies refuse to grant any assistance, some sceptical journalists even suggested my role as a government spy pretending to do academic research. Notwithstanding all the obstacles, I am delighted that I did not give up, but took pains to chug along, and finally persevered. I managed to collect to the best of my ability the necessary data for this project over an extended span of two years.

The publication of this dissertation would not have been possible without the suggestion and encouragement of Professor James Curran. The project idea germinated with my discussions with Professor Jan Servaes. The dissertation was completed under the supervision of Professor Chin-Chuan Lee. Professor Thomas Hanitzsch helped me with the conceptual framework. Interviews with foreign correspondents in Beijing, Shanghai, and Hong Kong were conducted from late 2015 to early 2018. I am deeply indebted to all of them.

I am especially grateful to my mentor Professor Chin-Chuan Lee, who shows me what academic rigour and a true scholar of social concern really mean. What I have learned from him will benefit me for life. My gratitude also goes to Mr. Mike Chinoy, Professor Cherian George, Professor Tianding Wang, Dr. Gerald Stell, Mr. Tian Chuan, and Mr. Liu Xiaochen for their generous help and support. This book also benefited from discussion with Professor Rasmus Kleis Nielson, Professor Henrik Örnebring, and Dr. Zvi Reich. Kitty Imbert and Margaret Farrelly from Routledge have been very helpful in moving the process of publication along smoothly. My special thanks to two China correspondents, Michael Forsythe and Ananth Krishnan, who helped to review my book manuscript. I am no less grateful to other journalists who graciously accepted my interviews, but for reasons of security I regret that I can only thank them collectively. Chapter 3 of this book is the revised version of a paper previously published in Journalism. I thank Sage for permission to republish the article.

I dedicate this book to my parents, whose unconditional love and support have been a source of strength and inspiration for me to live, respect, and explore the world with a heart for righteousness and eyes for fineness.

To

My parents

Zeng Xiancai and Zhao Jianping

1   Introduction

The first two decades of the 21st century are by any measure restive. The Western-orchestrated liberal global order is undergoing drastic changes, major established Western democracies burned with old and new threats ranging from the staggering economy, the rise of populism, and increasing distrust in the establishments to global security issues and climate change. Coupled with this shake-up, in the traditional Global South, China has risen to unprecedented significance in almost all dimensions and is still keeping its momentum on the rise. Its decades of blistering economic growth outshining other major economies and its growing assertive diplomatic stance have been drawing extensive global attention. It is not only described as the world's most populous country and the world's second-largest economy, but also as the emerging superpower, or the leader of a new world order. Meanwhile, at home, President Xi Jinping has been relentlessly tightening political and ideological control, further undermining press freedom and civil society, solidifying the illiberal autocratic governance of the 'China Model.'

The whole world is attentively watching China and looking for any hint at changes in the global order. Yet in media industry, fake news and the proliferating social media are further complicating the landscape of global journalism. Amid fear and bewilderment is a genuine need for a better understanding of the constructed reality. The foreign press corps in China play the important role of making sense of this mammoth 'other' for the global public and policy makers. Through selection and reinterpretation, foreign correspondents make daily occurrences into news cycles that shape the mediated reality of China.

By internalizing norms of reporting China, these foreign correspondents have morphed into key *agents* who interpret China for the rest of the world, operating in what Bourdieu calls a *journalistic field* in a transnational context. In Jean Chalaby's (1998) words, the journalistic field is a specialized and relatively autonomous field of discursive production with 'a tremendous impact on the discourse produced by the press'. While being semi-autonomously dominated and defined by internal norms and dynamics (journalistic logic), the journalistic field is also shaped by the political and economic powers in its immediate social space. It is in this relational and spatial power sphere that foreign correspondents enter the field within which they construct the news narratives on China. These news narratives in turn shape the societal level perceptions and conflicts.

Drawing on the conceptual framework of field theory and social structural constructivism, this book focuses on the dynamics internally and externally shaping the field of foreign correspondence in China during the first tenure of China's President Xi Jinping, from late 2012 to early 2018. The aim of this book is to unpack how foreign correspondents respond to pressures from within the journalistic field (such as a transforming media industry) as well as from the changing global geopolitics and China's increasingly restrictive media environment.

Perceiving China on the rise

The Chinese economy has transitioned from developing-country status to newly industrialized economy (NIE) status and is on its way to becoming a fully developed economy. Both the World Bank and the International Monetary Fund (IMF) forecast that, by 2030, China's economy will overtake the US, in terms of GDP, to become the world biggest economy.[1] A recent Pew Research Center poll shows that publics in Russia, Canada, Australia, and most European countries see China, instead of the US, as the world's leading economic power.[2]

Riding the wave of huge economic success, China has been trying to achieve more prominence, most notably on the diplomatic front. Steering away from the long-held 'hide and bide' (*tao guang yang hui*) doctrine adopted by Deng Xiaoping, the country is now crafting a much more assertive national image while seeking to gain pervasive influence on the world stage. China's President Xi Jinping, having scrapped the constitutional requirement on presidential office term, is abandoning the decades-old collective leadership established by Deng Xiaoping at home. Posing for a more centralized one-man rule, Xi has called on his country to head for 'the great rejuvenation of Chinese nation' and to attain the status of 'a global leader in terms of comprehensive national strength and international influence' by mid-century.[3] Pursuing national rejuvenation, China has been relentlessly building a China-defined network of regional and international institutions, including the Asian Infrastructure Investment Bank and the

New Development Bank. It also has begun to implement its most ambitious geopolitical expansion scheme, the 'Belt and Road Initiative,' which promises to invest an estimated $1 trillion or more in infrastructures in 60 countries. The scheme includes one-third of world trade and GDP, covering over 60% of the world's population (World Bank, 2018).[4]

The international community has been speculating on these moves. It is eagerly seeking to understand what a rising China means. Just a quick glance at the narratives of media and policy makers around the world would sketch out the ongoing global conversation about China: keywords evidently being 'rise,' 'threat,' and occasionally 'enemy,' or a 'destabilizing revisionist power.'[5] The American think tank National Endowment for Democracy coined the notion of 'sharp power,' proposing to gauge an aggressive China on the rise from the perspective of its extraterritorial influence – the pervasive coercion and manipulation China employs to quell unfavourable opinion worldwide. The US-led West is especially worried about the expansion of an illiberal Chinese model, which is posing as a 'dangerously appealing' alternative to Western-style liberal democracy, both in internal governance and international norms for other developing nations. *The New York Times* talks of a 'new Cold War' triggered by China. National Public Radio of the US produced a rarely seen special series of reports, entitled 'What an Emboldened China Means for the World.'[6]

As the world's only superpower so far, the US increasingly sees China as its biggest threat in both geopolitical and geo-economic domains. Pundits and policy makers refer to it as the 'most dynamic and formidable competitor in modern history.'[7] In its 2017 National Security Strategy, the Trump administration officially labels China as the 'strategic competitor' and a 'revisionist power,' which is trying to 'change the international order in their favor.'[8] In a speech delivered ahead of the mid-term election in late 2018, Vice President Mike Pence explicitly singled out China as the sole enemy of the Trump administration, pinpointing China's 'authoritarian expansionism.' As *The New York Times* points out, it is the first time a top American official delivered a narrative of Chinese aggression so publicly.[9]

In Australia, the Turnbull administration commissioned a report on Chinese influence, which, according to Australian media and pundits, was the main inspiration for the foreign interference law passed in 2017, Australia's most drastic addition to its espionage laws in decades.

It is difficult to measure the role of media in the current world perception of China and its assertive rise. Attempting to do so is beyond the scope of this book. But one can never overestimate the symbiotic relationship between news media and policy making. This could be epitomized by a quote from Vice President Mike Pence's latest speech on America's China policy delivered in October 2018:

> It's . . . great to see more journalists reporting the truth without fear or favor, digging deep to find where China is interfering in our society, and why. And we hope that American and global news organizations will continue to join this effort on an increasing basis.[10]

Alice in the wonderland of Middle Kingdom – the foreign press corps as mediator and sense maker

After its three decades of uninterrupted growth, China has arguably become an international news hotspot, attracting global journalists with 'a billion stories' (Osnos, 2013) and hailed as 'one of the wonderful places to be for a reporter, because it is both amazing and important.'[11] The case of foreign correspondence in China is part of foreign reporting in a globalized and networked journalism environment that makes sense beyond borders. A conduit for influence from policy makers, both domestic and foreign, foreign reporting is also a counter force to influence policy making, by not only providing world citizens with insights into a mediated reality 'foreign' to them, but also affecting foreign policy. As Ebo (1997) notes, 'the international image of a nation as articulated in the international media is an important assessment of the acceptance or impact of a nation's foreign policy in the global arena' (p. 47).

Yet in the increasingly interconnected globe where the public can have access to transnational information through various channels, the foreign news hole in general is shrinking (Emery, 1989; Hannerz, 2004; Hachten & Scotton, 2011). Global media conglomeration in pursuit of maximum profit has also contributed to the withering of foreign correspondence. Coping with what Sambrook (2010) calls 'structural changes,' the profession of foreign correspondents has 'evolved to flourish' (Hamilton & Jenner, 2004). With the interconnectedness brought by globalization and new technology, the value of foreign correspondence is shifting from providing timely information to providing interpretation as sense makers. Consumers of foreign news understandably lack background knowledge about a distant foreign nation to make sense out of a news story as news makers expect they do. They need a professional guide or 'curator,' as how an NPR Beijing correspondent terms their role as foreign correspondents, to walk the public through the knotted net of contextualized information and meanings.

Geographically vast, culturally diverse, and ideologically remote as China has been for foreign correspondents, there is never easy interpretation of this Middle Kingdom. Paul French (2009) likens foreign correspondents trying to get sense out of China to Lewis Carroll's Alice: as Alice in Wonderland, foreign correspondents come to China carrying their own looking glass and expectations, shaped by their previous life experience; these looking glasses and expectations, together with the 'twists and turns on the journey' (p. 3), shape their news production practice. The practice of an individual foreign correspondent or individual news outlet should be understood in the larger context of both the news outlets where foreign correspondents are employed and other interacting institutions outside news outlets per se, with proper consideration of the dynamics affecting journalistic practice at both the organizational level and the institutional level. Only with more knowledge on this could we understand how the wandering Alice makes sense of the wonderland of the Middle Kingdom.

Since China's opening up to foreign press in the early 1980s, news organizations from major countries have been steadily maintaining their presence in China. In the past five years, the foreign press corps operating in China has counted around 600 journalists.[12] The strong presence especially from countries such as the United States, Britain, and Japan, remains notable, even amid the global decline of foreign correspondence. These news organizations of various national origins are competing in Beijing, where the political system remains rigidly authoritarian and the Leninist-style control of party journalism prevails. This illiberal political and media system in China restricts foreign press not only by directly exerting pressure and coercion, but also by nurturing what Qian and Bandurski (2011) call an 'information vacuum' (p. 56). The government's strategy of muzzling China's own press complicates the dynamics of foreign reporting in China in a context where foreign correspondents are becoming increasingly important to convey to the world happenings in China. There has been, for example, a noticeable decline of investigative journalism in China following the decade-long 'golden period' that preceded Xi's coming to power (Svensson, Sæther & Zhang, 2014). Compared with the past decade, in which investigative journalism and civil society in China were relatively flourishing (see e.g. de Burgh, 2004; Hassid, 2011; Lee, 2006; Tong, 2011), foreign journalists are now increasingly being relied on to mediate and make sense of China.

Faced with the paradox of a significant China and a repressive reporting environment, foreign correspondents fight for their positions where they reconcile and interpret China for their audience at home, helping to frame the world's understanding of China and thus contributing to shaping international relations. Especially in the internet age, foreign media coverage plays a large part in shaping public discourse in China by being circulated back into China. These factors make the field of China correspondence a particularly interesting case to build up and unpack foreign reporting. China's rise may provide China correspondents with better-than-ever organizational resource support and make it easier for them to mobilize interest from both audience and editors. Additionally, entry restrictions may foster diversity and competitiveness, as more individuals are trying to secure a position in the field. But the intensifying competition within the field potentially results in changes on the power relations, for example, with external pressures.

Structure of the book

Drawing on Bourdieu's notions of *journalistic field* and habitus, this book aims to build up a conceptual framework of 'the field of foreign correspondence' and to tap on the changing structure and dynamics of foreign correspondence in a rising China. The defining power relations in the field of foreign correspondence are multifaceted, boiling down to political controls, economic incentives and pressures, media cultures, organizational newsroom controls, journalistic routines, and the individual dispositions journalists carry into the field. These forces work together to relationally define the news production practice and shape the final news product. It is, however, not within the scope of this book to exhaust the discussion of the dynamics that shape foreign journalists' news production. Instead, the book limits its focus to three broad perspectives: the habitus of individual journalists, journalistic logic including newsroom control and routines, and political control and media culture. Economic and technological factors, admittedly vital sources of influence, are not the primary focus of the discussion here.

To understand the practices of agents in a field of, say, news production, one needs to understand not only the structure of the field and the habitus of individual agents, but also how the whole field is situated in relation to the broader field of power. Bourdieu defines the three levels of analysis in field study:

> First, one must analyze the position of the field vis-à-vis the field of power. . . . Second, one must map out the objective structure of the relations between the positions occupied by the agents or institutions who compete for the legitimate form of specific authority of which this field is the site. And, third, one must analyze the habitus of agents, the different systems of dispositions they have acquired by internalizing a determinate type of social and economic conditions, and which find in a definite trajectory within the field under consideration a more or less favorable opportunity to become actualized.
>
> (Bourdieu and Wacquant, 1992, p. 104)

These three levels of analysis organize the structure of this book. The following chapters aim to describe the current configuration of the field of China correspondence, the habitus of China correspondents, and how they internalize journalistic logics, against the backdrop of external factors including the restrictive media culture in China and their own home cultures. The overall discussion is also expected to provide some empirical evidence to help situate the field of China correspondence between the autonomous pole and heteronomous pole in the broader field of power.

Besides contextualizing the topic of this book in a changing global order with an increasingly assertive China rising as the leader of a new world order, this introductory chapter intends to lay out the theoretical framework of this study – 'the field of foreign correspondence.' Chapter 2 sketches the institutional boundaries, historical trajectory, and configuration of the field of China correspondence, by explaining the party-journalism culture in China and how generations of foreign correspondents have evolved reporting China in the past seven decades since the founding of the People's Republic of China (PRC). This chapter is also an introduction to the journalistic field in China and to the external dynamics (i.e. China's oppressive media culture and tight control on foreign press) that define the field of foreign correspondence in China. In the 'New Era' as called out by President Xi Jinping, China correspondence has also entered the 'new era' of reporting a rising and assertive China, following the successive stages in the past decades widely referred to as 'red and virtuous China,' 'liberal China,' and 'repressive China.' The boundaries of the field are becoming permeable thanks to globalization and new ICTs, yet at the same time further institutionalized under strict laws and regulations. The nation-state context of the news organizations operating in China and the geographic spread of these news outlets both configure an imbalanced structure.

Chapter 3 delves into the habitus of individual journalists as the starting point for further scrutiny on the dynamics and structure of the field of China reporting. It describes how different sorts of habitus bring individuals into the field and land them into different positions. The habitus of China correspondents are unpacked into demographic properties, categories of 'journalistic habitus' (professional role perception, professional education, work experience, etc.), and 'Chinese habitus' (Chinese-language proficiency, China-related experience, etc.). By so doing, the morphology of modern-day China correspondence field is pictured, and a habitus-based typology for China correspondents is proposed ('globetrotting *Spiralists*,' '*Sporadics* on short overseas stint,' '*Sinophiles* caring about China more than about journalism,' and '*Sinojournos* committed to both China and journalism'). This chapter also forms the basis for a subsequent discussion on how correspondents holding different sets of habitus respond differently to the pressures within and outside the field or to the existing power structure. Chapters 4 and 5 examine the journalistic internal dynamics of the field. Chapter 4 looks at this journalistic logic at the organizational level, focussing on professional training as a newsroom control and the relational positions and autonomy of China correspondents in the news organizations. Distant from editorial desks and headquarters where organizational control is usually centred, foreign correspondents are widely considered as elites in the journalistic profession who enjoy high autonomy. This chapter debunks this myth by scrutinizing the autonomy that China correspondents enjoy in organizational contexts and the organizational control from newsroom socialization, resource allocation, and reporter-editor covenant. It acknowledges that China correspondents enjoy relatively high autonomy, but the degree of autonomy varies with the different positions of correspondents and news organizations.

Chapter 5 continues this endeavour within the journalistic logic, but goes beyond organizational boundary. It examines the collective reference practice by China correspondents, who in effect form an 'interpretative community,' and how this community is going ambient thanks to the prevalence of digital technology especially (social media) and inter-media mutual validation of a shared discourse. It weighs on the practice of collective reference as the unavoidable product of positional pressure. Journalists in different positions negotiate their autonomy with external pressures, and either differentiate or de-differentiate themselves from peer journalists as their important reference group. This chapter argues that the routine practice of press review as collective reference is a professional necessity, largely defined by colocation and nationality. But 'collective reference practice' is not necessarily 'pack journalism,' this chapter argues, as the former is a journalistic professional necessity due to positional pressure in the journalistic field, whereas the latter, as in its widely employed critical connotation, is the negative yet unnecessary result of the former.

Chapter 6 looks at the increasingly aggressive state coercion as a major disruptive external force on China reporting and how China correspondents negotiate with these pressures. State coercion in China, encompassing both 'stick and carrot,' is manifested in, among other things, access blockage, harassment, and flak. Although China correspondents have developed countermeasures, including exposing harassment and anticipatory avoidance, none of these measures addresses the structural conditions. The power structure is hardly challenged, with the 'anaconda in the chandelier' continuing to be writhing in the field and threatening the journalistic practice of China correspondents.

The concluding chapter, Chapter 7, discusses and reflects on the three key perspectives of dynamics both within and outside the field of foreign correspondence: the habitus of individual journalists, the journalistic logic in newsrooms and in the press corps as an interpretative community, and state coercion of the host country as well as different media cultures. It looks back at the various power relations that structure the field of China correspondence, as identified in preceding chapters, and summarizes the external non-journalistic pressures, as well as the innate social and cultural gap, as the 'unreportability' of this rising authoritarian China. While acknowledging the still prominent heteronomous pressures that are cramping the autonomy of the field of China correspondence, the study reports on a tendency, even though only partial and mild, towards a globalized journalistic culture within the globalization in the broader social space.

Conceptualizing the field of foreign correspondence

News is a knowledge made in a certain paradigm that reinforces and justifies the ideological boundaries (Bourdieu, 1994; Gans, 1979; Molotch & Lester, 1974; Reese, 1990; Tuchman, 1978; van Ginneken, 1998). News-workers make news out of daily occurrences within specific ideological boundaries to dish out a 'media reality' to audiences, and new occurrences rise in response to these 'realities,' which are then filtered into another round of 'mediated realities' (Lang & Lang, 1955). Among others, Gans (1979) provides an exemplary sociological account of how all participants in the newsmaking process – journalists, sources, audience – collaborate and negotiate to 'decide what is news' and how the news is reported.

News production is thus a structural construction, a collective enterprise that is undertaken through collaboration in various forms. In the new media ecology, citizen journalism empowered by new information and communications technologies (ICTs) is gaining increasing momentum, as citizen journalists work together with traditional journalism professionals to shape a social reality provided by news media. This increasingly networked endeavour in the ever-changing political economy requires more spatial perspective in journalism study.

Bourdieu (1993, 1996) uses the concept of '*field*' to refer to the power relations in the social space where *agents*, whose *positions* in the field are defined by their habitus (systems of dispositions) and the *capital* they possess, compete or struggle with each other for social, economic, cultural, and symbolic capital, the accumulation of which would steer them into more advantageous positions in the field. A field thus forms a social space of competition and alliances between agents (Neveu, 2007). The concept of field does not only unpack any cultural production analysis into interrelated layers of individual producers (habitus of agents) and the position (structure within the field), but also its relation to economy, politics, and culture (the position of the field in the broader field of power); most importantly, it locates the analytical focus in a historical and structural context, emphasizing fluidity and reflexivity.

In conceptualizing the notion of field in relation to cultural production, Bourdieu did not specifically address 'journalistic field' until in his late academic life (1998, 2005):

> Journalism is a microcosm with its own laws, defined both by its position in the world at large and by the attractions and repulsions to which it is subject from other such microcosms.
>
> (Bourdieu, 1998, p. 39)

Bourdieu locates the journalistic field in broader power relations with other fields and forces, to emphasize the structural construction of news. It spans a continuum ranging from a heteronomous pole, where economic (pressures from audience and advertisers) and political power is dominant, to an autonomous pole, where cultural power is dominant. The introduction of the field approach into media studies is championed by scholars including Benson (1999, 2005), Neveu (2005, 2007), Hesmondhalgh (2006), and Couldry (2003), for its merit of placing journalism in a relational and dynamic social space, thus departing from the tendency toward media-centrism (Lindell, 2015). Van Ginneken (1998) also subscribes to this view by noting that news making is a consensus of intersubjectivities, which are 'always situated and shaped socio-historically' (p. 19). The field approach bridges the analytical divide between the macro-sociological level of structural factors and the micro-sociological level of organizational factors (Dickinson, 2008). It also bridges between agency and structure.

Bourdieu and his followers mainly argue for the decreasing autonomy of the journalistic field from the economic field and how this weakened autonomy of the journalistic field is influencing public life. This may be because, as Champagne (1995, cited by Benson, 1999) notes, in Western democracies, political power is less visibly exerted on the media than economic power is. In authoritarian societies, political power is much more directly exerted, and in cross-national reporting, the political realm exerts a more visible influence, via international geopolitical wrestles and political control in both the host country and the home country of the newspeople.

Benson (2005) developed Bourdieu's under-elaborated notion of journalistic field by detailing the pressure emanating from the political field, structural-ecological properties, and historical path-dependent processes. Other researchers using or critiquing Bourdieu's somehow crude notion of journalistic field also acknowledge the importance of political power (Darras, 2005; Schudson, 2005).

Foreign correspondence, taken as such a field, is interwoven and interacting with economic, political, technological, and cultural fields in a complex cross-national context. Rather than in a single nation-state context. It draws on power relations both in the host and home countries and across national borders. For example, journalists born in China and educated in Britain may work for American news media operating in China. Working for different news organizations of various national contexts, these journalists acquire certain habitus, or values and preconceptions, through what van Ginneken (1998) identifies as 'threefold socialization': cultural, professional, and organizational. They seek and take on their own *positions*, which are the legitimized and institutionalized social conditions of news production in the field. They interact and negotiate in multiple power relations with other players ranging from sources, audience, peers, and editors to regulators, political actors, interest groups, etc. from both their home country and host China, from both within and outside the field of foreign correspondence. It is the ensemble of dynamics in and among these relational power struggles that define foreign correspondence in a specific host country.

The journalistic field, in Bourdieusian terms, spans a hierarchical ladder co-constituted by multiple diverse fields, including the cultural production field and the larger field of power (i.e. the combination of economic and political fields). The national journalistic field is also situated in the global social space. Thus, it seems that the structural location of the field of foreign correspondence can be conceptualized as a twofold hierarchy: one of the journalistic field nested in the economic and political fields and one of the foreign correspondence field vis-à-vis the national journalistic field of host and home countries, all of which are situated in a global journalistic field. In other words, the study of foreign correspondence involves the structural position of a hierarchy of individual journalists, news organizations, and the journalistic field in the host country, in home countries, as well as globally.

Field perspective is still rare in comparative foreign correspondence studies. Benson (2006) and Hallin (2005) applaud using the notion of journalistic field to underscore cross-national differences. For example, Benson (2006) compares the 'political/literary' French journalistic tradition and the 'informational' American journalistic tradition and argues that the comparison helps to map out the 'variable qualities of the field and field configurations' (p. 86), including the external and internal economic organization, the restrictive or enabling role of the state (as in the narrow sense of 'political field'), historical trajectory, level of autonomy, and internal morphology and demography of the field.

Journalists as *agents* in the field have the primary shaping power on social reality, which has been eloquently argued in earlier classical studies (see e.g. Breed, 1955; White, 1950). The notion of habitus or *dispositions* in Bourdieusian terms refers to their demographic characteristics, educational background, prior life and career experience, values and beliefs in the profession, and values and beliefs in general. The habitus shapes their different positions, which legitimize their power and capital in the field. For example, journalists with higher education and richer experience practicing with elite media outlets (who possess more capital) would have a better chance of occupying higher status and by implication a more autonomous position in the field, which in turn legitimizes their symbolic capital (which can be translated into more substantial capital). Journalists cooperate and compete with each other, driven by what Bourdieu calls 'positional pressures' (1998, p. 49), which shape their routine practice such as collective reference, i.e. press review, and potential homogenization of the final news product.

Routinized practices are norms passed down in or across newsrooms along the historical trajectory of journalism as a profession. New entrants pick up these routines as unquestioned rules to resist external pressures in the field, thus securing their positions. Both Hallin (1992) and Høyer (2005) observe that contemporary journalists have better internalized the basic norms of journalism, which now have traveled across borders.' These widely accepted journalistic norms not only mirror the historical account of tensions between the journalistic field and the external pressures, but also reflect the current structural position of the field, and especially that of the newsroom in the field. Besides, the bureaucratic structure of the news organizations in the field also works to shape the position of the individual journalist in the news organization and how much editorial autonomy the journalist enjoys. Journalists with more autonomy, or 'star journalists', face different pressures than do those with less autonomy.

Various institutional players in both host and home countries work together with foreign journalists to form a networked media space, where sources, audience, other news organizations, advertisers, and state actors (through regulations, governing, and other forms of political pressure such as state coercion) all take part in the process of news making (Breed, 1955; Corcoran & Fahy, 2009; Reese & Danielian, 1989).

Media cultures in each national context are shaping the field of foreign correspondence largely via shaping the journalistic habitus during the socialization process of individual journalists. For example, in comparing the national journalistic fields in France and the United States, Benson (2005) notes that French journalists are more concerned with 'expressing their opinion' than in digging up 'facts,' compared with their American peers (p. 98). These, as in path independency, are the impact from national journalistic fields of home countries onto journalists who are professionally socialized in these distinct national journalistic fields and which formed their journalistic habitus.

Hallin and Mancini's (2004) analysis in their seminal work *Comparing Media Systems* identified four key dimensions of media system: commercial media market, political parallelism, professionalism, and state intervention. These four dimensions in effect measure the degree of autonomy of the journalistic field from the economic and political fields, thus echoing the field perspective of autonomy in the broader power field. Their concept of *media system* is hence borrowed to operationalize media cultures of the national journalistic field of each country as a key variable in conceptualizing the field of foreign correspondence, which is detailed in the following methodology section.

Data collection

All the empirical data this study is built on are drawn from surveys and in-depth interviews I conducted with former and current China correspondents from November 2015 to August 2018. These first-hand data are complemented by existing records by China correspondents, professional groups, and researchers. The combined methods are to garner the most resources available, as such social science research is not encouraged in today's highly political-sensitive China and official information about foreign press is intentionally not made publicly available. It is also expected to compensate for the low response rate of China correspondents, who do not always give the benefit of doubt to me, a then PhD student and Chinese national.

This study does not involve newsroom observation, one of the traditional methods in journalism studies. This is mainly because foreign correspondents work in very small-sized newsrooms. A large number of them are one-person bureaus, with the exception of a handful of large news wires (e.g. Reuters, Kyodo News, Agence France Presse) and leading American newspapers (e.g. *The New York Times*, *The Wall Street Journal*). Therefore, the newsroom in foreign reporting is becoming permeable and no longer the most rewarding focal point to observe journalists' work, which is mostly done outside a newsroom.

The survey was implemented from October 2015 to April 2016, asking the respondents about their demographic characteristics, working routines, role perception, and perceived influence on their journalistic work. The whole population of foreign correspondents effectively registered in mainland China at the time with a valid email address provided by the 'Foreign Press Directory' issued by China's Ministry of Foreign Affairs is selected for the survey ($N = 604$). By the end of 2016, altogether 101 valid responses were collected. The response rate is 16.7%.

The respondents are from news organizations of 25 countries, which are regarded as the 'home country' of China correspondents. These 25 countries are grouped into four clusters following a revised Hallin and Mancini's (2004) typology of media systems: the Liberal Model countries (US, UK, Canada, Ireland, Australia),[13] the Democratic Corporatist Model countries (Germany, Finland, Denmark, the Netherlands, Sweden, Norway, Switzerland), the Polarized Pluralist Model countries (France, Italy, Spain, Colombia), and non-Western countries.[14]

The response rate is admittedly low. It is not just what Wilnat and Weaver reason as 'the transient nature of foreign correspondents' (2003, p. 410) that makes it especially difficult to have a satisfyingly large size of sample. The sensitive time during which the study was undertaken should also be duly considered to have a full picture: foreign correspondents are highly alert of the ever-tightening media control in China and especially the pervasive state surveillance on them. As a journalist working with a US newspaper told me, they suspect the Chinese government tactfully spies on them using the cover of academic research.

Yet some assurance can be gained by a chi-square goodness of fit test (see Table 1.1) which shows little significant deviation ($p > .05$) of the distribution of the sample in terms of country of origin (by the news organizations the journalist works for). Some small misrepresentations are observed, such as the under-represented number of non-Western journalists, which is largely attributed to the low response rate of Japanese correspondents (sample $N = 8$) who form the largest national group among foreign correspondents in China ($N = 117$).

Table 1.1 Spread of Sample across Country

Country of News Org	Observed N	Expected N	Residual
Liberal Countries	36	32.9 (197)	3.1
Democratic Corporatist Countries	20	17.1 (102)	2.9
Polarized Pluralist Countries	18	15.3 (91)	2.7
Non-Western Countries	27	35.8 (214)	−8.8
Total	101		

$\chi^2 (2, N = 101) = 3.429, p = .33$

Twenty-three semi-structured in-depth interviews with former and current China correspondents were conducted from November 2015 to August 2018 in Beijing, Shanghai, and Hong Kong. These interviews ran from 50 minutes to 120 minutes, averaging just over one hour. Permission to audio-record the interview was granted in all cases, but the identities of some interviewees are withheld, upon their request. By country of origin, of the 23 correspondents who accepted to be interviewed, two are from Indian news organizations, three from German news organizations, 10 from American news organizations, six from international news agencies, one from Colombia, and one from Turkey.

Conclusion

How to make sense of China's assertive rise and its global impact during the 'New Era' of Xi Jinping's leadership has become a widely discussed yet gravely under-researched topic for both policy makers and academia. Foreign press as the primary mediator and sense maker of China is the focus of this book, which aims to contribute to the understanding of a rising China that is closely relevant to global readers.

China's strictly controlled media environment and its increasing global prominence are the fundamental pair of dynamics that are driving various power struggles in China reporting by foreign press. How they cover China on the rise and shape debates and global perception of China is the question I aim to explore in the following chapters.

I borrowed Bourdieu's notions of field and habitus to construct the framework of 'the field of China correspondence.' This field framework offers the advantage of a relational and spatial perspective to examine foreign news production in the mesh of the habitus of individual journalists, journalistic logic including newsroom control and routines, and political control and media culture. It bridges the agency and structure in journalism studies, situating journalists in habitus-and-capital-based positions, *shaped by* the tension between journalistic logic from within the field and non-journalistic logic exerted from external fields of power, meanwhile *shaping* the whole power structure of China reporting. The notion of 'the field of China correspondence' also helps to situate the news production by foreign press in a broader global context of media culture and geopolitical wrestle.

Notes

1 IMF Country Focus: China's Economic Outlook in Six Charts. Retrieved from https://www.imf.org/en/News/Articles/2018/07/25/na072618-chinas-economic-outlook-in-six-charts

2 Wike, R., Poushter, J., Silver, L., & Bishop, C. (2017). Globally, More Name US than China as World's Leading Economic Power. Pew Research Center, 13. See www.pewglobal.org/2017/07/13/more-name-u-s-than-china-as-worlds-leading-economic-power/
3 As laid out in Xi's speech on CCP's 19th National Congress held in late 2017. Link in Chinese: www.xinhuanet.com/politics/19cpcnc/2017-10/19/c_1121823252.htm
4 World Bank (2018). Belt and Road Initiative. See https://www.worldbank.org/en/topic/regional-integration/brief/belt-and-road-initiative
5 An example would be a Bloomberg opinion piece headlined: "How China went from a business opportunity to enemy No.1". See https://www.bloomberg.com/opinion/articles/2018-09-06/how-china-went-from-a-business-opportunityto-enemy-no-1.
6 Barma, Naazneen H. and Ely Ratner. 2006. "China's Illiberal Challenge." *Democracy: A Journal of Ideas* Issue 2, Fall 2006: 56–68; Perlez, J. (February 27, 2018). Xi Jinping extends power, and China braces for a new cold war. *The New York Times*. Retrieved from https://www.nytimes.com/2018/02/27/world/asia/xi-jinping-china-new-cold-war.html; Dobson, W. (October 2, 2018). *China unbound: what an emboldened China means for the world.*
7 Campbell, K. & Ratner, E. (2018). The China Reckoning. *Foreign Affairs*. Retrieved from https://www.foreignaffairs.com/articles/china/2018-02-13/china-reckoning
8 The White House. (December 2017). National Security Strategy. Retrieved from https://www.whitehouse.gov/wp-content/uploads/2017/12/NSS-Final-12-18-2017-0905.pdf
9 Landler, M. (October 3, 2018). Pence speech to string together a narrative of Chinese aggression. *The New York Times*. Retrieved from https://www.nytimes.com/2018/10/03/us/politics/china-pence-trade-military-elections.html
10 Remarks by Vice President Pence on the Administration's Policy Toward China. Retrieved from https://www.whitehouse.gov/briefings-statements/remarks-vice-president-pence-administrations-policy-toward-china/
11 About 'networked journalism', see Beckett, C., & Mansell, R. (2008). Crossing boundaries: New media and networked journalism. *Communication, Culture & Critique*, 1(1), 92–104; Heinrich, A. (2011). *Network Journalism: journalistic practice in interactive spheres*, New York: Routledge.
12 This figure only includes official registered journalists and does not take into account the many unregistered freelancing journalists.
13 Australia is added to the Liberal Model group for its pattern that closely follows British political, economic, and media institutions; for the same reason, Colombia is grouped into the Latin tradition of Polarized Pluralist Model (Hallin & Papathanassopoulos, 2002).
14 Hallin and Mancini's (2004) original typology only taps on Western democracies. Considering the distinct journalistic culture shared among non-Western countries (Hanitzsch et al., 2010; Voltmer, 2012), as well as the fact that correspondents from non-Western news organizations are much smaller in number, I group all Asian countries (excluding Australia), Eastern European countries, and Middle East and African countries into one category: non-Western.

2 Confrontation and obedience

When foreign journalists meet Chinese media culture

Rodney Benson (2005) rightly pinpoints the importance of understanding the historical emergence and evolution of the journalistic field. In order to better grasp the boundaries and dynamics of the present-day field of China correspondence, a close look into the trajectory and social context of reporting China would thus be helpful. China's illiberal media culture might be the most important social context for analyzing the field. Known for its strong tradition of party-media system in which media are held to function as the mouthpiece of the party (Zhao, 1998, 2012), as well as for its highly restrictive media controls (Liang, 2002; Shirk, 2011), China and foreign, especially Western, press have long been on tense terms. The non-governmental press watchdog Reporters Without Borders ranks China 176th out of 180 countries in their 2018 World Press Freedom Index. Meanwhile, as Chinese media are facing increasingly tightened censorship, foreign media are becoming an important source of information in China, to the extent that internet users in China half-jokingly share a saying: Learn English language to better understand China (*xue hao ying yu, liao jie zhong guo*). In other words, the foreign news media are needed for accessing news stories that would otherwise have been censored in Chinese media.

This chapter aims to present a contextual and historical overview of the formation and evolution of the field of China correspondence. To that end, it sheds lights on the illiberal media culture of China and the socio-historical trajectory which shaped the present-day boundaries and configuration of China reporting.

Party journalism: China's unwelcoming media culture

Running contrary to the Anglo-American journalistic tradition, which emphasizes the media's role as a public service and the 'Fourth Estate,' China's media system began to morph under Mao in a context ideologically dominated by Leninist press theory (Zhao, 1998, 2012). Though having showed some sign of liberalization since adopting market reforms in the 1980s, China's media system reverted to the Soviet censorship model following the failed democracy movement in 1989. From the mid-1990s to late 2000s, the Chinese press experienced a 'golden period,' when watchdog journalism flourished against the backdrop of marketization and relatively loosened party control (Tong, 2011). Yet the party-state has never been fond of the idea of a free media, and the primary context remains the party-journalism apparatus. Even Hu Yaobang, the most reform-minded leader of China, who was purged in 1987 and died two years later, triggering the pro-democracy movement in Tiananmen Square, describes the role of party journalism as 'the mouthpiece of the Party.'[1]

Under the leadership of Xi Jinping, the reporting space of the Chinese press has been further squeezed by a combination of the party's tightening grip on media and civil society, financial pressures, and digital challenges (see e.g. Cook, 2016; Tong, 2019). The deterioration of China's media climate is illustrated by the relatively liberal newspaper *Southern Weekly*'s New Year editorial incident in 2013, when the paper's annual editorial advocating constitutionalism was censored and brazenly replaced by a completely different one penned by the provincial top propaganda official (Wong, 2013). Ensuing large-scaled protests by journalists, intellectuals, and even ordinary citizens and celebrities ended to no avail. The incident is seen as the beginning of a harsh winter for Chinese press and a strong signal that the Xi regime aims to intensify media censorship (see e.g. Wu, 2005).

As if to affirm the new leadership's unyielding resolve to gain full control of the media, the first five years into Xi's office witnessed a relentless crackdown on media and civil society, manifested by the closing down of media outlets and social media sites, and harassment or imprisonment of journalists.[2] At the beginning of 2016, Xi made a rare tour of the Beijing headquarters of the three major state media, *People's Daily*, Xinhua News Agency, and China Central Television (CCTV), where he explicitly demanded 'absolute loyalty' to the Party, asking all party media to 'bear the last name of the Party,' and to 'speak for the Party's will and its propositions and protect the Party's authority and unity,' as well as to 'align their ideology, political thinking and deeds to those of the Party, and focus on positive reporting only.'[3] The blunt reaffirmation of China's party journalism by the all-powerful Xi, who is unmistakeably engaged in centralizing all power to establish an autocracy, is, as I see it, both rhetorically and normatively running counter to the doctrine of independent journalism whose 'only loyalty is to the democratic process itself' (Carey, 2001, p. 24).

Party journalism in China is increasingly centred on consolidating the legitimacy of the Chinese Communist Party's (CCP's) rule. To borrow from Hallin and Mancini's (2004) four-dimension analytical toolkit, China's media system is defined by political parallelism and lacks professionalism, while its mass media market component is as yet not fully developed. It is heavily controlled by the ruling CCP, while displaying 'the highest level of political instrumentalization' (Zhao, 2012, p. 161). To further tighten its control over media, the Central Propaganda Department of CCP was granted sweeping powers in early 2018 to supervise and regulate all media platforms in the country.[4] In the journalistic field, the department's jurisdiction encompasses most of the major state media, and it comprehensively supervises and censors all Chinese news media. It issues editorial guidelines and directives to censor sensitive topics, to ensure that all media outlets heed the Party's policy (see e.g. Xu, 2014).

China's party-journalism culture has had a strong impact on how foreign correspondents operate, especially those who are steeped in liberal media traditions in which public service journalism and professionalism are highly valued. In a host media culture that emphasizes the role of the media as a government mouthpiece and 'positive reporting,' foreign correspondents not only find themselves constrained by stringent entry restrictions and limited access to news sources and information, but they also face political coercion and public distrust in the overall repressive media climate and subdued civil society of China. The public in China, accustomed to the 'positive reporting' practiced by the mammoth party-journalism apparatus, is not hard to convince that foreign media are 'biased' and engaged in smearing campaigns against China by their critical coverage, when often foreign media, especially Western media, produce a China narrative that is distinctively different from the national narrative that Chinese party journalism constructs. The Party's official mouthpiece *People's Daily* published on its website a study entitled 'Demystifying How Western Media Smear China,'[5] and another one with the headline 'Why Are Western Media Smearing China?'[6] Both are penned by Chinese scholars. Meanwhile, another national newspaper published by the state-run Xinhua News Agency criticized *New York Times*' coverage of China's Belt and Road project as 'smearing China' and 'ill-intentioned.'[7] Xinhua denounced the notion of 'sharp power' as Western media's new tactic to smear China.[8] Such an unwelcoming media culture in China almost assures confrontation with foreign press.

Historical trajectory: a brief history of reporting from China

The history of foreign reporting, especially Western reporting from and about China, traces its origins to the 1820s, when the first batch of foreign correspondents landed in China. Since then, China reporting has witnessed the decline of the feudalist Qing and the rise of the Nationalists, followed by the rise of Communist China.

After CCP came to power in 1949, China expelled most Western correspondents and allowed only a handful of 'CCP-friendly' journalists to remain (Chu, 1984). Farmer (1990) recounts that not one foreign correspondent was on site in Beijing to cover the historic moment when Mao Zedong announced the official establishment of the People's Republic of China. By the mid 1960s, Communist China was so isolated that only Reuters, Agence France Presse, the Toronto *Globe and Mail*, and some Japanese news outlets still had one or two correspondents stationed there (Hohenberg, 1967). Until China's opening up in the 1970s, the country was practically out of reach for the foreign press. Liang Jingdong (2002) wrote that during the decades between 1949 and early 1970s, the eve before the normalization of relations between China and the US, no American journalist could make their way through the 'Bamboo Curtain' as a reporter. Only after 1979 could foreign media organizations for the first time develop an actual presence in the country. The bloodshed of the Tiananmen crackdown in 1989 structurally changed the dynamics of China's domestic politics and of China reporting by foreign media. China shifted to a less liberal outlook, while the bloody crackdown became a 'collective memory' (Lee & Chan, 2016), which cast China as repressive (Li & Lee, 2013). Since the beginning of the new century, a mixed concern for 'China's rise,' synchronized with an influx of foreign news organizations and journalists, set the stage for a more diverse news discourse. The dynamics of China reporting has again undergone changes with the advent of Xi Jinping, driven by his increasingly aggressive diplomatic policy and domestic authoritarian governance, against a backdrop of drastically changing global power relations.

Before 1970s: unimportant and distant red China

During the Cultural Revolution from 1966 to 1976, foreign media had to observe red China from the outside, from Hong Kong, Tokyo, Bangkok, or even their home desks. China reporting during this period largely consisted in analyzing and interpreting official handouts and other second-hand accounts from mainland refugees and foreign business people visiting China (Chu, 1984). The vacuum in China reporting lasted until the 1972 Ping Pong tournament, which marked the point when China gradually began to open its doors to the international community. As a result, Western media were allowed to set foot on the soil for the first time since the beginning of the Cold War. American journalists saw in it a 'golden opportunity' to see and report the 'mysterious land' (Chu, 1984). Hoping to steer American public opinion away from supporting Taiwan, as well as to enlist sympathy against the Soviet Union, the Chinese government embarked on a comprehensive propaganda campaign targeted at foreign journalists. Meanwhile, the US was seeing in China an ally fighting against the Soviet Union. This alignment of interests left a mark on US media coverage of human rights abuses in the Soviet Union and China, which tended to show a favourable bias when dealing with the latter (Harding, 1990; Lee, 2002).

These journalists came to China with little knowledge of this culturally and ideologically distant country. Few of them in the 1970s had systematically studied China before their China assignments. Instead, they largely relied on the Maoist propaganda apparatus as a source of knowledge on their host country. Besides, against the background of domestic social movements in the US, many of these American journalists were themselves left-leaning activists holding high hope for the communist model. For example, in the 1960s and 1970s, American correspondents' sympathies toward China were tied to their opposition to US involvement in the Vietnam War and domestic social injustice at home (Song & Lee, 2016). Because of the structural constraints (highly restricted information access and the US's national interests both politically and economically), as well as their own dispositions (left-leaning, lacking sufficient knowledge on China), they portrayed China during the radical Cultural Revolution as a romantic new China with 'material progress through self-reliance,' a pre-industrial society with 'high purpose and morality' and equality (Song and Lee, 2014).

Late 1970s–late 1980s: liberal China going capitalist

After the Cultural Revolution, with the debut of economic reform and opening-up policy, China gradually opened its door to foreign media. In 1981, China issued for the first time formal regulations on foreign media, requiring all resident foreign journalists to apply and register with the Ministry of Foreign Affairs. All foreign journalists were required to be based in Beijing only and to apply for permission to interview any group, company, or institute, while renting office space and local hiring had to be commissioned to Chinese agencies. Later in 1983, 29 more cities were opened up for foreign correspondents without a travel permit, yet the requirement to report to the local foreign affairs department was maintained (Chu, 1984).

Taking advantage of Beijing's cautious overtures, the American press corps, firstly led by the Associated Press, followed by CNN and NBC, promptly opened China offices, and foreign journalists have been able to regularly work and report in China ever since. China correspondents came into being in this fresh configuration.

During this period until 1989, US media coverage on China had distanced itself from the Maoist revolutionary news frame. Instead, it showed sympathy with Deng's rhetoric of economic reform, perceiving China through the lenses of the American-universal values, cheering for marketization, and continuing to downplay human rights topics (Song & Lee, 2016). This somehow cheery 'liberal China going capitalist' paradigm came to an abrupt halt when the bloodshed of the Tiananmen crackdown in 1989 shocked the over-optimistic West. The failed democracy movement in China echoed the drastic political changes that rocked the world in 1989, heralded by the fall of the Berlin Wall. This was a time when foreign correspondents, especially American correspondents, heavily engaged with the incidents that they were supposed to cover, as many of them sympathized with the students in the pro-democracy movement and expected the movement to have political consequences.[9] After the crackdown by China's hardliners, many foreign journalists were expelled. But some of them built their career reputation on covering Tiananmen, such as *New York Times'* Nicholas Kristof and Sheryl WuDunn, awarded the 1990 Pulitzer Prize. Photojournalist Jeff Widener of the Associated Press, parachuted into Beijing from Bangkok, shot the iconic 'Tank Man' photo, for which he was nominated as a finalist for the 1990 Pulitzer Photography Prize.

Post-Tiananmen: repressive China depicted with caution

After the turmoil of the Tiananmen crackdown in 1989, whose foreign media coverage remained a cause of embarrassment for the Chinese government, China tightened regulations on foreign media. The 1990 government regulations on foreign press were the strictest, by not only requiring rigid permission application procedures,[10] but also by explicitly stating for the first time the penalties that foreign journalists were liable to incur in case of any 'violation.' Additionally, these new regulations explicitly prohibited freelancers from operating in China.

The aftermath of the Tiananmen crackdown has been haunting China's politics, as well as foreign correspondents covering China, who became very sensitive to topics related to repression, press freedom, or human rights in general. China reporting 'descended into the abyss of despair,' as foreign correspondents, afraid of repeating the mistakes of misjudging the democracy movement in 1989, tended to refrain from predicting China's prospects and thus adopted a repressive frame to hedge their journalistic claims (Mann, 2001; Song & Lee, 2015). Another reason for the then-pervasive repressive frame, as Wakeman (2001) notes, is that such stories were proven to be more attention-grabbing for the audience of foreign media, especially for American television viewers.

Globally, the end of the Cold War dramatically changed the world order from bi-polar into the US-led 'new world order.' The US-China alliance against the Soviet Union consequently lost its reason for being, as China took over from the former Soviet Union as the 'new enemy' of the US (Lee, 2002). This shift in global power structure, coupled with the legacy of the Tiananmen crackdown, drove foreign journalists into a more cautious and critical view of China. Though they covered a wide range of topics from the continued economic reform and rapid growth to environmental deterioration, inequality, and moral vacuum (Peng, 2004), they constantly drew on stock images of the bloodshed to construct a repressive story frame during the post-Tiananmen decade (Wakeman, 2001). The legacy of 1989 has left an enduring mark on the way that foreign media cover China (Lee, Li & Lee, 2011), a mark which remained visible well beyond the 1990s. Kristof, mentioned earlier, is now a columnist for *The New York Times* and still writes about the Tiananmen crackdown on its anniversary.[11]

Rising and powerful China – a 'new era'?

These strict regulations lasted until the eve of the 2008 Olympics in Beijing, when the State Council issued the new *Regulations of the People's Republic of China on News Coverage by Permanent Offices of Foreign Media Organizations and Foreign Journalists.*[12] These regulations brought one major change in that foreign journalists no longer require government permission for their reporting activities; they only need to get prior consent from the interviewees. This change was widely acclaimed as a major breakthrough in the process of loosening the media environment and making it more accessible to the foreign press (though it later proved to have little effect). In addition, the foreign press is given more freedom to hire Chinese nationals for non-journalistic work.

Since the late 1990s, China has been cautiously promoting a benign image of itself as 'peaceful rise' (Zhu & Lu, 2013). But in Xi Jinping's 'New Era,'[13] both China's domestic policies and global significance have undergone a noticeable change. It is growingly perceived as an eminent challenger not only to the US but also to most major countries and to its close neighbours such as India, Japan, and other Asian countries. China's huge overseas investments, especially in Africa, have been bashed as 'neo-colonialism' (Zhu & Lu, 2013). Against the backdrop of social problems such as terrorism, the refugee crisis, and the rise of populism in major Western countries, especially after 2016, 'the rise of China' is often contextualized as synchronized with 'the decline of the West.' Meanwhile, the debate over the so-called China Model became a global subject. Foreign correspondence in China is seen as having entered a 'new era,' which could be taken as the fourth phase of foreign reporting in China, attentively focussing on China's challenge to the post-1945 global order in a more mixed and realistic tone.

Lee (2010) observes that the Chinese government has been eagerly attempting to remove the stain of the Tiananmen crackdown by emphasizing economic growth and nationalism as the main sources of its legitimacy. Xi Jinping's leadership has been mobilizing the imagery of economic growth and nationalism, while anti-corruption campaigns have been used as a third source of political legitimacy. Especially after China's economy started to show signs of recession in 2015, the new leadership made moves to introduce a new style defined by an assertive foreign policy while significantly tightening ideological control at home. The previously pursued 'peaceful rise' diplomacy has now veered towards a quest for 'discursive power on the global stage' (Lee, 2016, p. 102).

In the past two decades, the size of foreign press stationed in China has been increasing significantly. The number of registered foreign correspondents in China jumped to 480 in 2005 (Qian, 2012), up from 170 in 1990,[14] and peaked during the Beijing Olympics in 2008 at around 700. Its size remained stable at around 600 ever since, a figure that includes many journalists from non-Western countries. The increase in the number of correspondents on the same posting, together with the rapid development of China's economic power and global presence, understandably bring changes to the dynamics of the field. Former CNN Beijing Bureau Chief Jaime Flor-Cruz terms foreign media's depiction of China in the new era as marked by 'diversification.'[15] This book specifically examines the field of China correspondence in this 'new era.'

Institutional boundaries of the field of China correspondence

To map the boundaries of the journalistic field, one needs to define the entry delimitation of agents, not only those autonomous rules and regulations of the profession per se, but also those that are institutionally imposed on the field. To this end, I introduce below the institutional definition of the concept of 'China correspondents.'

An institutional definition of China correspondents

As Bourdieu (1983) notes, 'every literary field is the site of a struggle over the definition of the writer' (p. 321), so is the definition of foreign correspondents as the news writers in the field of foreign correspondence. To accurately define foreign correspondents is the first step to understand the boundaries of the field, which sets the entry delimitation for individuals striving to become such an agent, and is 'a stake of struggles' with 'extreme permeability' (Bourdieu, 1983, p. 322).

According to traditional definitions, a foreign correspondent is distinguished from a journalist in general, either as 'a journalist who works in a state different from the one in which his information-medium is located' (Marx, 1970 in Hahn & Lönnendonker, 2009, p. 56) or as a special species in the journalistic profession with an advantageous position, typically as 'a cosmopolitan among cosmopolitans, a man in gray flannels who ranks very high in the hierarchy of reporters' (Cohen, 1963, p. 17), 'the princes of the profession' (Yemma, 2007), enjoying relatively high autonomy (see e.g. Morrison & Tumber, 1985).

But such traditional boundaries have been challenged by struggles with external power led by the proliferation of globalization and new ICTs. Internet-based technologies are making it easier for editors at home to extend the newsroom control to foreign correspondents abroad; citizen reporting, made possible by social media, is encroaching the space traditionally occupied by foreign correspondents. The rapid and vast media conglomeration that places profit above all other considerations and the loss of appetite for international news after the end of the Cold War also contribute to the changing ecology of foreign correspondence.

These new changes led some scholars to argue that foreign correspondents as a species are waning (Merle, 2013; Willnat & Martin, 2012) or that they have evolved into a more diverse and less elite species, including 'traditional foreign correspondents' and 'new foreign correspondents' such as freelancers and bloggers (Hamilton & Jenner, 2004). Individuals with less economic and cultural capital compared with traditional foreign correspondents are seen getting into the field as 'new foreign correspondents.'

The competition among individuals for legitimate positions in the field is getting tense, as China assignments are endowed with more symbolic capital for a journalist compared with the last century when the country was of less significance. New generations of journalists equipped with a better cultural understanding of China are entering the field, visibly making the boundaries of the field more competitive and demanding for individual agents. The 'traditional correspondents' and 'new correspondents' are mobile and interchangeable in the field of foreign correspondence. 'New foreign correspondents' (freelancers, bloggers, etc.) is in fact one of the two main career paths for foreign correspondents.[16] A large number of traditional foreign correspondents come from positions as freelancers, who work their ways into an economically and socially more secured traditional correspondent position. Foreign correspondents meanwhile extensively rely on these non-traditional foreign correspondents for information and connections, and they sometimes become freelancers themselves.

In the case of China reporting, ever since the beginning of the contemporary field of China correspondence in the 1970s, the boundaries of the field, though with intermittent relaxation, have remained rigidly institutionalized. China correspondents are strictly monitored through institutionalized accreditations. Access to information is tightly restricted, and even local fixers whom foreign correspondents traditionally rely on as an indispensable extension of their own limited local knowledge and connections are kept under highly centralized management. Under tight control, the traditional foreign correspondents in Hamilton and Jenner's typology are still the major players in China.

For these reasons, I am turning to the institutional definition of China correspondents for analysis. The United Nations Convention on the International Right of Correction sets an exemplary institutional definition of foreign correspondent as an individual employed by a media organization who is regularly engaged in the collection and the reporting of news material and who, when abroad, is identified as a correspondent by a valid passport or by a similar document (*Convention on the International Right of Correction*, 435 U.N.T.S. 191). The definition applies in China, where foreign correspondents are officially defined by China's Ministry of Foreign Affairs as 'career journalists who are dispatched by foreign media organizations to be stationed in China for a period of no less than six months for news coverage and reporting' and explicitly codified through laws and regulations.[17]

Setting the boundaries institutionally: regulations on foreign correspondents

Foreign media and foreign correspondents in China are subjected to regulations from at least six government units: the State Council Information Office; the State Administration of Press, Publication, Radio, Film, and Television (SAPPRFT); the Ministry of Industry and Information Technology; the Cyberspace Administration; the Ministry of Foreign Affairs (MOFA); and the Ministry of Public Security. Of these units, MOFA is the immediate and principal supervisor for foreign press in China. In 2000, China set up the International Press Center under MOFA to exclusively manage and facilitate foreign correspondents' accreditations, reporting activities, and daily issues.[18] Local public security bureaus and foreign affairs offices are also major actors in regulating journalistic activities in their realm and enforcing the above regulations.

The current version of *Regulations of the People's Republic of China on News Coverage by Permanent Offices of Foreign Media Organizations and Foreign Journalists*[19] state that both news organizations and journalists need to get approval from the MOFA for operating in China. All resident foreign journalists, once approved, shall register with MOFA or local foreign affairs offices within seven days of arrival to be issued a Press Card, after which they are required to register with the public security authority for a residence permit. In addition, a resident foreign journalist needs to stay in China for no less than six months on an accumulative basis, or his/her Press Card is liable to cancellation. Foreign news outlets in China can employ Chinese nationals only for 'auxiliary work.' When carrying out any reporting activity in China, foreign journalists are required to carry either their Press Cards (in the case of resident foreign journalists) or a Journalist Visa for Short Visit (J2 visa, in the case of a 'parachute journalist'). But for a temporary J2 visa, journalists are required to submit applications 30 days in advance. This rule practically paralyzes the practice of parachuting in journalists for breaking news.

Though still strictly confining, this latest regulation is substantially relaxed compared with the previous 1990 version, which required official approval from local governments for any reporting activity. However, the seemingly relaxed regulations do not apply in all parts of China. The autonomous region of Tibet, for example, is strictly controlled, only occasionally allowing organized visits by foreign journalists. Meanwhile, in practice, foreign reporters complain that the regulations 'never translated into changes in reality,' as local officials outside Beijing or Shanghai are reported continuing the old practice of rejecting foreign journalists, citing 'lacking permission from Foreign Affairs Office,' as if the new law had never been passed down to the provincial level (PEN America, 2016).

This suggests the strong retention of social practices shaped via old, though officially nullified, laws and regulations. Especially when new regulations are intentionally made vague and leave room for interpretation, the dynamics and tension in the field cannot be changed structurally. Reuters Beijing correspondent Paul Carsten is not alone among the foreign press corps in commenting that 'rules are so vague that obviously it works in the favour of the authorities because they can interpret them however they need to in any given situation.'[20]

Other regulations and rules are aiming at directly or indirectly restricting foreign media's information access. One example is SAPPRFT issuing in June 2014 a directive to Chinese journalists warning of punishment if they pass information to foreign journalists.[21] Similarly, the *Law on Management of Domestic Activities of Overseas Non-governmental Organizations*, effective since January 2017, requires overseas NGOs operating in China to register with the Ministry of Public Security or its local bureaus and to not engage in any fundraising in China. Additionally, they are not allowed to fund Chinese organizations from overseas.[22] This move was widely regarded as a further clampdown on civil society in China and signalled Chinese authorities' 'determination to repress unwelcome foreign influences and activities that foster the spread of "Western values"' (Lubman, 2015). The closing up of both domestic and foreign NGOs serves to squeeze the field in which China correspondents routinely rely for sources.

To respond to the new internet-based publishing ecology, China also issued draconian and ambitious rules and regulations to administer cyberspace, promoting an authoritarian mode of 'Internet sovereignty'[23] that is completely at odds with the 'free speech, free internet' mode familiar to most Western journalists. In February 2016, SAPPRFT and the Ministry of Industry and Information Technology jointly issued the *Online Publishing Service Administration Rules* with new regulations on online content by a foreign company, in effect forbidding foreign media from publishing any online content in China without prior approval. The latter would only be issued to those partnering with Chinese companies and who have their servers inside China, such as to bring them into conformity with Chinese laws and regulations.

However, similar restrictions on foreign online content providers have been seen before. *The Wall Street Journal* interprets that 'gathering them together in a single regulatory scheme allows Beijing to cite a legal justification for its intensifying drive to fortify Chinese society, particularly the Internet, against what the authoritarian government sees as unwanted foreign influences' (Chin, 2016).

To recapitulate, the boundaries of the field of China correspondence are institutionally defined by a set of restrictive rules and regulations, even though the broader economic and social forces (such as globalization, ICTs) are permeating the boundaries of journalism (Lewis, 2012). At least in China reporting, open participation is still largely out of the picture; the option of entering the field is still strictly limited to professional journalists or, more precisely, to *licensed* professional journalists. These rigidly institutionalized boundaries of China correspondence effectively facilitate China's state control over the agents, as there is not much room for foreign journalists to negotiate with controls exerted via codified rules and regulations. Each individual ready to step into the field prepares him/herself for conforming to all the directly relevant regulations, via their predecessors in the newsrooms, professional organizations such as the Foreign Correspondents Club of China, and regulating bodies such as China's Ministry of Foreign Affairs; many China correspondents report being lectured on 'dos and don'ts while reporting in China' when being interviewed for the journalist visa application.

China correspondents tend to obey these codified regulations, as their accreditations depend on their obedience. In fact, at the local level, these foreign journalists sometimes find themselves using these codified regulations to negotiate reporting space with official disruptions. As aforementioned, the latest 2008 version of the regulations on foreign press and correspondents is clearly loosened up, at least in its literal sense; when local officials disrupt their work, correspondents on site would immediately object by citing clauses in the 2008 regulations or even by contacting MOFA officials in Beijing for help if their direct negotiation fails. But the help they could enlist from Beijing is becoming rare, as the field is entering the 'new era.'

Mapping the configuration of China correspondents

Between 2015 and 2016, the time of this study, there are more than 600 registered foreign correspondents in China. Which countries and news organizations are they reporting for? Where are they based in China? Answering these questions about the configuration of China correspondents provides a cognitive map for better analyzing the field, as the configuration, national, geographic, and organizational, inevitably contributes to shaping certain dynamics within the field and thus shaping journalists' practice of news production.

Imbalanced landscape of global news prism

In the field of China correspondence, we observe a clear centre-periphery structure in terms of the nation-state power balance in the global news prism, with most of the richly represented news organizations in China from industrialized G7 countries or other major Western developed countries. This echoes scholars' and international organizations' call to address the chronic malaise of the imbalanced global news flow (most famously addressed in the *MacBride Report*, 1980; also seen in e.g. Brüggemann et al. 2016; Kopper & Bates, 2011).

Among all foreign news organizations operating in China, the largest newsroom is Reuters, with 36 registered journalists based in Beijing and Shanghai, followed by the 17-person China reporting team of Agence France Presse. For non news wires, the largest China reporting team is Japan's NHK, with 14 journalists, followed by the *Wall Street Journal*'s 13-person newsroom. But these well-staffed news organizations are only a handful; a larger number could only afford one single staff correspondent in China.

Though foreign correspondents have long been depicted as cosmopolitan (Cohen, 1963; Hannerz, 2004), and many reporters and editors of 'international' news outlets refuse to be labelled as American or British organizations or anything with an obvious nation-state stamp,[24] they are nevertheless still 'a prime source for integrating cultural frames and ideologies into news flows' (Kopper & Bates, 2011, p. 53). National contexts are still essential differentiating variables that mark the lines segmenting the foreign press corps.

Foreign press corps in China is no exception. Of all the 47 countries with news outlets in China, the US and Japan clearly dominate the centre. Figure 2.1 shows that, in terms of size, the US and Japan are the top two countries with the largest reporting teams in China, with the US ranking first in newsroom number ($N = 37$) and Japan first in staff size ($N = 117$). The US has the highest number of news outlets in China, which is consistent with US media's dominant role in the global news prism. Japan is not as prominent in the global news prism as the US or even Britain, but as one of the

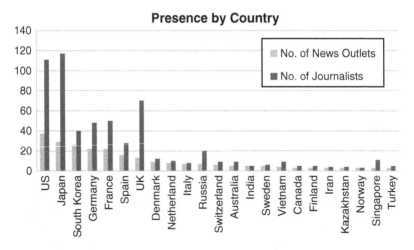

Figure 2.1 Size of Foreign Reporting Teams in China by Country (2015–2016)

major developed countries and a G7 member country, its leading presence in China still echoes Van Ginneken's (1998) assertion that a limited number of G7 media companies basically control the transnational flow of news.

After the US and Japan, South Korea, Germany, France, and the UK can be categorized as the second tier as to the size of their media presence in China, with more than 40 journalists from each country. Apart from Japan and South Korea, both of which are prominent Asian neighbours of China, all others taking the lead in presence in China are major Western countries.

Such an imbalanced landscape has a considerable impact on the practice of China correspondents within the field. A typical example is the Indian press in China, apparently on the periphery. There are altogether only five Indian correspondents, all based in Beijing, each representing one English-language Indian media outlet, from a country with the second-largest population and the fastest growing major economy.[25] The long-term tense yet important bilateral relationship between the two Asian rivals is feeding Indian media's coverage on China. During the tensest Doklam standoff between Indian and Chinese armies in the summer of 2017, Indian newspaper readers could hardly find China stories that were not related to the standoff. One of the many reasons is that the five Indian correspondents have to devote their time fully to getting the China Foreign Ministry's response on a daily basis, which left them little time to write on other topics. One of them complained that he had hit his own record for attending the Foreign Ministry's daily press conference in a row for almost a month.[26]

The imbalanced landscape, paired with the diverse media systems of each country and their distinct national interest with China, highlight the complex dynamics of the field of foreign correspondence in a nation-state context. The comparative context of national-level influence is introduced in each of the following chapters, which tackle power relations at different levels.

Beijing and Shanghai: centre of China

Morrison and Tumber (1985) reminded us that news is where newsmen/women are. The geographic location of bureaus is an indicator of the structure of institutional power relations, as news organizations tend to base their limited number of staff correspondents in places where most sources and resources are. Chinese regulators also require foreign news organizations to base their China bureaus in a handful of large cities for easier supervision. Therefore, one also observes a clear centre-periphery structure in terms of the geographic spread of foreign newsrooms in China: The more than 600 registered China correspondents are scattered in major megacities, from Beijing (77.8%) to Shanghai (19.6%), and a small number reside in other large cities, including Guangzhou and Shenzhen in southern China, Shenyang and Dalian in northeast China, and Chongqing in mid-west China, showing a clear-cut centre-periphery structure, with Beijing and Shanghai as the undisputed centres.[27]

The map in Figure 2.2 visualizes the 'peripheric' parts of China, such as less economically developed western China, which are largely ignored by foreign press. To echo this geographic spread of foreign correspondents in China, the Foreign Correspondents Club of China also operates in Beijing and Shanghai.

Beijing, the capital city, is the political and cultural centre of China; it is also the magnet of China's intelligentsia, with the largest number of universities, think tanks, and research institutes in China. In the early 1980s, the foreign press was required to open their offices in one of two designated hotels in Beijing (Qian, 2015). For decades, it has been where journalists' routine sources prevail: central government press briefings, official proceedings, national ceremonial events, and the like. Other regular sources such as government officials, academics, and China experts are also mostly found in Beijing. Not to mention that the city itself is a news generator house, attracting foreign correspondents to write on its food, culture, air pollution, and of course the social malaise reflected in the tensions in this capital city.[28] With the best public infrastructure and the second-largest number of foreign residents in China,[29] it is also one of the most accommodating cities to live in China for expatriates. Van Ginneken (1998) observes that a large foreign community is also an important consideration for the selection of geographic location of overseas bureaus for foreign media, as they favour a more congenial environment with similar cultural values and ideological affinities. For example, South Korean news organizations in Beijing mostly open their offices in the Wangjing area, nicknamed 'Korean Town,' where around 30,000 South Koreans are based.[30]

Foreign journalists in Beijing enjoy the convenience of numerous international schools for their young children, high-end supermarkets where they can find imported goods from their home countries, and weekends hiking on a wild section of the Great Wall and posing for a picture on top of the great world wonder.

Beijing is the news hub not only of China, but also of Asia. For many small media organizations which could only afford dispatching one correspondent to cover the entire Asia or part of this vast land, most likely this 'Asia correspondent' would be based in Beijing. This is both for the newsworthiness of China and for logistic concerns – China imposes stricter regulations on foreign press than do most other countries in the region, thus it is sensible

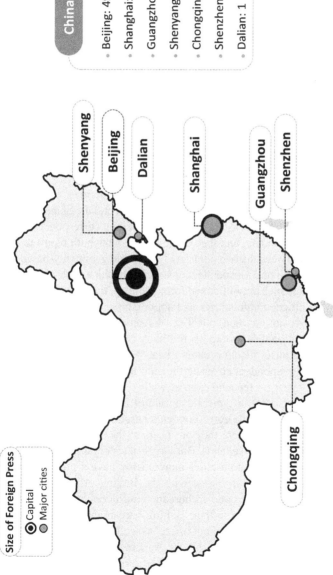

Size of Foreign Press
● Capital
● Major cities

China: 639

● Beijing: 497
● Shanghai: 124
● Guangzhou: 11
● Shenyang: 3
● Chongqing: 2
● Shenzhen: 1
● Dalian: 1

Shenyang

Beijing

Dalian

Shanghai

Guangzhou

Shenzhen

Chongqing

Figure 2.2 Map of Foreign Press in China

for a foreign correspondent to apply for a resident journalist visa for China and fly out to cover other neighbouring countries occasionally, rather than trying for days or even weeks to parachute into China from outside, even from Hong Kong.

Beijing is usually the priority choice for any news organization that aims to open a China bureau, whereas as China's financial centre, Shanghai understandably serves as the ideal base for news organizations and journalists specializing in business and financial news, though now it is losing its appeal, with news outlets generally withdrawing their overseas reporting team.[31] Once the 'Paris of the Orient' in the colonial period and the Asian hub for foreign correspondents until 1949, Shanghai still maintains its unique culture of relative openness and diversity, hailed as the most cosmopolitan city for expatriates in China (Hewitt, 2001).

Between Beijing, Shanghai, and nowhere: labour division and cooperation

For news organizations with correspondents in both cities, no hierarchical line necessarily exists between the Beijing bureau and the Shanghai bureau. The German radio broadcaster ARD has one Beijing correspondent and one Shanghai correspondent, and the two correspondents both report to editors in Germany. Between the two, they have beats- and geography-based labour division: the Beijing correspondent covers north China with Mongolia and all general beats such as politics and foreign policy; the Shanghai correspondent covers all economic stories and south China, including Hong Kong. The division is not codified, but it can be rigid. For example, the annual Beijing International Auto Expo is routinely covered by the Shanghai correspondent, because 'it's an economy beat.'[32] *The Wall Street Journal* has a Shanghai correspondent covering the auto industry, and he is flown into Beijing every year for the auto expo as well.

In the case of ARD, a typical example of one-person bureaus in both Beijing and Shanghai, the correspondents based in the two cities in effect form a virtual office, where they are peers at the same hierarchical level and take duty shift on weekends. But larger news organizations with more staff correspondents in both cities unavoidably have a more hierarchical structure between the two bases, with the Beijing office almost always the superior, both in size and in bureaucratic hierarchy. *The Wall Street Journal* has 10 journalists in their Beijing bureau and three in Shanghai; Beijing serves as both its 'Beijing office' as well as 'China bureau,' led by its China bureau chief Charles Hutzler. Agence France Presse has 15 journalists in Beijing, including chiefs,[33] correspondents, editors, and video and photo journalists, but only one correspondent and one photographer in

Shanghai; the only Shanghai correspondent reports to Beijing Bureau Chief Patrick Lescot, as well as to Asia editors in Hong Kong.

This geographic layout and subsequent beat division of foreign press in China unavoidably affect their access to sources and understanding of China, even when they are physically *in* China. China is a vast land with a population of 1.4 billion, unevenly distributed between the east coast and the west inland, between rural and urban areas. Basing correspondents only in megacities projects a totally different image of China than would basing them in a county in northwestern China undergoing urbanization or in a minority ethnic village in southwestern China striving to maintain its traditional heritage. Just think about how Washington DC-based American media and pollsters overlooked the non-college white constituency in rural America in the 'bizarre' US presidential election in 2016 (Cross, 2018).

For a closer look at the impact of geographic location of newsrooms on media coverage, I compared 44 articles filed by the *Wall Street Journal*'s Beijing and Shanghai bureaus in January 2017.[34] These articles cover four beats: political/general ($N = 13$), economy ($N = 14$), market ($N = 5$), and companies ($N = 12$). The Beijing bureau apparently covers most of the political/general news, ranging from foreign policy (e.g. China's new move in the South China Sea) and China's domestic politics (e.g. gun-related crimes in China) to social news in general (e.g. public discussion on which side to stand on an escalator); the Shanghai bureau contributed more than 40% of its 14 stories to the company beat. All but one of the datelines of these 44 articles were filed from either Beijing or Shanghai. Only one article on Facebook's China business was co-filed from Beijing, San Francisco, and Wuzhen, a small town in China's richest Zhejiang province near Shanghai, known for hosting China's annual World Internet Conference.

Admittedly, geographic constraints on news coverage could be more prominent for smaller newsrooms with very few staff correspondents (such as in the aforementioned case of Indian news outlets) than for *The Wall Street Journal*. But even for the latter, the impact on news coverage is easily noticeable:[35] the only story on social news filed by the whole China

Table 2.1 Topical Distribution between BJ and SH Bureau of WSJ in January 2017

Bureau	N (%)	Political/general news	Economic news	Market news	Company news
Beijing	30 (68.2)	11 (36.7)	10 (33.3)	3 (10)	6 (20)
Shanghai	14 (31.8)	2 (14.3)	4 (28.6)	2 (14.3)	6 (42.9)
Total	44 (100)	13 (29.5)	14 (31.8)	5 (11.4)	12 (27.3)

reporting team of the *Journal* is about the public debate on which side to stand while one is riding an escalator in Beijing's subway.[36] This typical metropolis perspective reflects how geographic constraints on journalists can gravely narrow the scope of their topic selection. 'Expatriate' journalists are mostly narrowly focusing on the discussion of foreign policy and national policies in Beijing and monetary and business trends in Shanghai. Even when they consciously, divert their attention to some 'life style' areas, they see shared bicycles, unmanned retailers, and mobile payment, all of which are only shared experiences in these limited urban areas with considerably higher economic indicators and more technology savvy residents, or they see the debate over which side to stand on an escalator, as in the case of *The Wall Street Journal*.

Conclusion

This chapter looks at the overall landscape of China correspondence, mapping out its cultural context, historical trajectory, institutional boundaries, as well as configuration. This is the prerequisite for understanding and further analyzing the conflict-driven power relations in the field, where foreign correspondents both confront and abide by the restrictive reporting environment in China.

A brief retrospect of the trajectory of foreign correspondence in China shows that both the agents and the power structures (national interests, information access, etc.) in the field have been changing, hence the changing news paradigms in covering China. Situated in different stages of historical development, journalists' habitus also shapes what Gans (1979) calls 'enduring values' or what Bennett (1990) alternatively terms 'myth structure,' which fundamentally helps to construct the China news narrative. Considering these historical heritages is essential to understand the present-day field of China correspondence, especially the one in Xi's New Era.

The paradox of China's economic prowess and tightened political authoritarian control is the first challenge that China correspondents reconcile. China's illiberal media culture, mostly embedded in the party-journalism apparatus, can be pinned down into two broad categories when analyzing its toll on foreign press. One is the institutional factors of government regulations and state coercion, which include codified regulations such as credentials control,[37] regulations restricting access to sources and information.[38] The other is a set of uncodified coercion and censorship mechanisms ranging from official flak and access blockage to harassment and surveillance.[39] The uncodified coercion will be discussed in length in Chapter 6.

Admittedly, though the global power structure is undergoing change, the whole landscape of the global media prism is still rather imbalanced, presenting a clear-cut West-dominant transnational news flow. Such imbalanced structure is also observed in the field of China correspondence, both in the nation-state context of the news organizations operating in China and in the geographic spread of these news outlets.

Notes

1 Hu, Y. (August 14, 1985). On the party's journalism work. *People's Daily*, p. 1.
2 Shen Hao, the former publisher of editorially liberal 21st Century Media, was sentenced to four years on allegation of extortion (Liu, 2016); Wang Xiaolu, a reporter with a renowned business magazine, was arrested on the charge of spreading false information in 2015; investigative journalist Liu Hu, on reporting a local official's corruption, was arrested and charged for defamation in 2013; there are many other cases of journalists detained without trial.
3 See (in Chinese) http://www.xinhuanet.com/politics/2016-02/21/c_128737586.htm
4 Li, P. & Shepherd, C. (March 21, 2018). China tightens grip on media with regulator reshuffle. Reuters. See www.reuters.com/article/us-china-parliament-media/china-tightens-grip-on-media-with-regulator-reshuffle-idUSKBN1GX0JG
5 Qu, X., Su, X. & Li, J. (May 23, 2012). (in Chinese) Western media work with their governments to smear China. Retrieved from http://world.people.com.cn/GB/17958583.html
6 Zheng, R. (August 8, 2017). (in Chinese) Why are Western media smearing China? Retrieved from http://media.people.com.cn/n1/2017/0808/c40606-29455410.html
7 Chong, S. (July 4, 2018). (in Chinese) Smearing China, Western Media Slap Themselves. Cankao Xiaoxi. Retrieved from http://column.cankaoxiaoxi.com/2018/0704/2287945.shtml
8 Wang, Y. & Li, X. (February 9, 2018). (in Chinese) Fabricating New Words to Smear China. Retrieved from http://www.xinhuanet.com/zgjx/2018-02/09/c_136961045.htm
9 Mike Chinoy's documentary series 'China Assignment' reveals many backstage stories of American journalists' illusion and disillusion while covering the Tiananmen crackdown.
10 Foreign journalists need to get permission from local foreign affairs offices for any interview activity.
11 See, e.g. Kristof, N. (June 3, 2009) Bullets over Beijing. *The New York Times*, Retrieved from https://www.nytimes.com/2009/06/04/opinion/04kristof.html?_r=1
12 English version of the regulations is published on the website of International Press Center of China, retrieved from http://ipc.fmprc.gov.cn/eng/wgjzzhzn/t716835.htm
13 The catchphrase 'New Era' first appeared in Xi's speech on the 19th CCP National Congress in 2017, to specifically refer to Xi's rule since 2012.
14 Liu, J. (December 1, 2006). (in Chinese) Ministry of Foreign Affairs Press Conference. Retrieved from http://www.gov.cn/gzdt/2006-12/01/content_459087.htm
15 Personal communication, December, 2015.
16 The other career path is being a staff reporter at a metro desk and assigned to an overseas posting after years of experience as a national or metro reporter.
17 *Regulations of People's Republic of China on News Coverage by Permanent Offices of Foreign Media Organizations and Foreign Correspondents.*

18 See the International Press Center's website: http://ipc.fmprc.gov.cn/eng/aboutipc/
19 For the full text, see http://ipc.fmprc.gov.cn/eng/wgjzzhzn/t716835.htm
20 Personal communication, February, 2016.
21 Full text of the regulations (in Chinese) retrieved from: www.gapp.gov.cn/news/1656/211765.shtml
22 Full text of the regulations (in Chinese) retrieved from http://www.xinhuanet.com//politics/2016-04/29/c_1118765888.htm
23 Starting from 2010, China issued the first white paper on the internet, in which the notion of 'Internet sovereignty,' which became the core agenda for China's 'authoritarian Internet regulatory model' (Jiang, 2010), was formally outlined. By advocating that national sovereignty should be applied to cyberspace, it asserts that 'within Chinese territory the Internet is under the jurisdiction of Chinese sovereignty,' a further attempt to legitimize its grip over cyberspace. This notion was further proclaimed at the first and second Wuzhen World Internet Conference held in December 2014 and 2015 respectively. See www.miit.gov.cn/n1146290/n4388791/c4638978/content.html
24 The ownership of news corporations is growing increasingly cross-national, lending a stronger sense of 'global media' or 'international media,' where correspondents are reluctant to identify themselves as 'foreign correspondents' anymore. Reuters used to be easily categorized as 'British,' but it ceased to be so after it was purchased by an American corporation. *Financial Times* is owned by a Japanese company. Ted Turner, the founder of CNN, is widely quoted as strongly opposing the use of the word 'foreign' in 'foreign correspondent.' No CNN correspondent reporting outside the US should view him/herself as a 'foreigner' to the host country; a better label would be 'international correspondent.'
25 According to IMF, Indian has overtaken China since 2017 to become the fastest growing major economy in the world. See https://www.imf.org/en/Countries/Infographics/APD-REO-2017/India-fast-growth
26 Personal communication, July, 2017.
27 The geographic expansion of resident correspondents in China is visible in the past five years. Acting in response to Chinese President Xi Jinping's geopolitical expansion programmes, news organizations are opening new bureaus beyond the traditional bases of Beijing and Shanghai, expanding to send journalists to reside in cities such as Guangzhou or Shenzhen in Southern China, with a clear focus on the robust technology industry in the area. British paper *The Daily Telegraph*, followed by Reuters, for example, opened their first ever South China bureaus in Shenzhen in 2017 and mid-2018 respectively; American TV network CNBC International is hiring a staff journalist to open a new bureau in Guangzhou, at the time of writing.
28 Examples of such news stories are *The Telegraph*'s report on a popular Beijing street food 'Chinese crepe' (https://www.telegraph.co.uk/news/2018/06/02/birthplace-chinese-crepe-fights-protect-authenticity-becomes/), *The New York Times*' report on the shouting hawkers in Beijing's old alleys (https://www.nytimes.com/2009/09/13/world/asia/13beijing.html), and NPR's report on Beijing's controversial policy of forcing out migrant labourers (https://www.npr.org/sections/parallels/2017/12/06/568315650/for-decades-chinas-laborers-moved-to-cities-now-they-re-being-forced-out)
29 According to the sixth National Census of China in 2010, Shanghai has more than 143,000 foreign residents, the largest foreign community in China, and Beijing has 91,128 foreign residents.

30 *Xinhua* (July 5, 2014). (in Chinese) South Korean in Wangjing: How Far is Beijing to Seoul? Retrieved from http://www.xinhuanet.com/world/2014-07/05/c_1111473908.htm
31 The *LA Times*, *The Washington Post*, and many other major news outlets have closed their Shanghai offices in the past two years.
32 Personal communication with the ARD Shanghai correspondent.
33 AFP has one Beijing bureau chief and one Beijing deputy bureau chief.
34 The month of January was randomly selected to analyze one month's coverage on China. All samples are retrieved from Factiva.
35 It would be ideal to choose the *New York Times*' coverage as an analysis of the difference in topical distribution between Beijing and Shanghai, as it is a more general paper compared with the *Journal*, which is a financial newspaper. But the *Times* had no correspondent in Shanghai between early 2015 and 2017. It used to have one Shanghai bureau chief, David Barboza, but he left China in early 2015 for an investigative article he wrote in 2012 on the family wealth of then China under threats Prime Minister Wen Jiabao (Chinoy, 2015). China has been denying visas to the *Times* correspondents since the story was published in 2012 (*New York Times*, 2012).
36 Chin, J. (January 10, 2017). How to ride an escalator: China says you're doing it wrong. *The Wall Street Journal*. Retrieved from https://www.wsj.com/articles/rising-risk-china-reconsiders-stand-right-walk-left-on-escalators-1484029173
37 Foreign journalists working in China are required to apply for a J visa and accreditations; both are renewed on a yearly basis.
38 Examples of such restrictive regulations: Chinese nationals are not allowed to work as journalists for foreign media; Chinese journalists are not allowed to pass information to foreign media; certain areas (Tibet) are not freely accessible for foreign journalists.
39 As detailed in Chapter 6, China uses its large and sophisticated internet filtering system Great Firewall to surveil and censor foreign media as well; other extra-legal sabotage activities including discrediting foreign media and detaining or harassing foreign correspondents.

3 China or journalism

Habitus and types of China correspondents

I want a reporter, someone who doesn't know the difference between an 'ism' and a kangaroo!

This is a line from Hitchcock's movie *Foreign Correspondent*. On the eve of World War II, the editor of an American newspaper is seeking to send someone as novice as a piece of blank paper to report from Europe. Fictional as the scene may be, it still is representative of a familiar debate that has lived in the field of foreign correspondence for decades: what individual qualities, be it expertise on the topic covered or language skills, make some journalists more preferred than others? A hidden assumption behind the debate is the argument that individual dispositions of journalists make a difference in journalistic practice. Be it the well-debated and extensively applied 'gatekeeping theory' or in what Mills (1963) criticizes as 'molecular' approach, individual newsworkers' personal beliefs and values are widely held for deciding what's news (Breed, 1955; Patterson & Donsbach, 1996; White, 1950). Their individual background characteristics, including education, family upbringing, professional values, and attitudes, work as what van Ginneken (1998) calls 'mental frames' or a 'yardstick,' shaping how news is constructed. Starck and Villanueva (1992) call it the 'cultural framing' of foreign correspondence, referring to how that foreign correspondent's education, professional experience, and linguistic and cultural competencies of the host country all contribute to the framing of the foreign reality to a home audience. In a similar vein, Hannerz (2004) avers that foreign correspondents tend to carry baggage from home to their overseas postings, and the baggage shapes how they view and construct occurrences into foreign news.

These individual traits constitute the habitus, a key construct developed by Bourdieu as his solution to the structure-agency dichotomy, which he dismisses as a false dilemma (Bourdieu, 1977; Dickinson, 2008). Bourdieu defines habitus as 'the mental structures through which they [the agents] apprehend the social world . . . a system of schemes of perception and appreciation of practices, cognitive and evaluative structures which are acquired through the lasting experience of a social position' (Bourdieu, 1989, pp. 18–19). It is 'an organizing principle of practices' (Neuve, 2007), thus is the starting point for understanding foreign correspondents' positions and practice in the field, as their position affects the degree to which it is in their interest to support or subvert the current structure of the field (Bourdieu, 1985; Handley & Rutigliano, 2012).

Journalists enter the field of China correspondence with different sets of habitus, which categorizes them into different positions in the field. Wacquant (2014) details three dimensions of habitus: cognitive (perception), conative (skills), and affective (desire, or the 'lustful dimension of habitus formation'). Following the three dimensions of habitus, I operationalize the habitus of China correspondents into components including the demographic characteristics, 'journalistic habitus' denoting professional experiences, beliefs, and interest, and 'Chinese habitus' encompassing life experience and knowledge on and interest in China. The construct of habitus as both conceptual and methodological tool is used throughout the book, and this chapter is specifically devoted to exploring the deconstructed habitus of present-day China correspondents and to proposing a habitus-based typology of China correspondents.

Demographics as primary habitus

Habitus as a socially embodied system of individual and collective dispositions is both natural and nurtured, thus it can be distinguished into *primary* habitus, which is generic, and *secondary* habitus, which is acquired through socialization in school or the workplace. The demographics of a group connote age, nationality, gender, and education, revealing much about the primary habitus of the individual agents entering the field. Field theorists have noted that demographic changes, including changes in the class composition of new entrants in the field, are crucial to examining the changing dynamics of the field (Benson, 1999).

The survey data provide the opportunity to picture the basic demographic dispositions of China correspondents, who are generally well-educated (97% of respondents hold a college degree or above) and experienced (with an average of 15.8 years working experience as a professional journalist), but also heavily male dominated (only 23.2% are women). They are mostly middle-aged in their 30s or 40s. Only two respondents are fresh college graduates in their early 20s.

Almost two-thirds of them have no connections to China, nor have they lived in China, prior to their China postings; 60% of them do not speak

Table 3.1 Demographic Characteristics

Sample Composition	Liberal	Democratic Corporatist	Polarized Pluralist	Non-Western	Total
Female	26.5%	25%	22.2%	18.5%	23.2%
Median Age	36–40	41–45	31–35	41–45	36–40
Years in journalism	14.2	19.9	12.7	16.9	15.8
Years in China correspondence	7.6	4.8	6.6	5.1	6.2
College educated or above	100%	95%	100%	92.6%	97%
Major in journalism	41.7%	30%	38.9%	25.9%	34.7%
Chinese fluent or above	58.3%	20%	22.2%	44.4%	40.6%
With prior foreign correspondence experience	75%	95%	94.4%	96.3%	88.1%
With prior China experience	55.6%	25%	33.3%	22.2%	36.6%
N	36	20	18	27	101

fluent Chinese, meaning a majority are not able to conduct interviews or research independently in Chinese. This relative unfamiliarity with China is acutely true for correspondents from Democratic Corporatist countries, of whom only 20% speak fluent Chinese and a quarter had lived or worked in China, or with other personal connections with China (such as born a Chinese national, being married to a Chinese, or having family in China), prior to their official China correspondent posting.

Male dominance

Consistent with almost any other research findings on the demographic characteristics of journalists (Hess, 1996, 2005; Weaver & Wilhoit, 1996; Weaver et al., 2014; Wu & Hamilton, 2004; van Dalen, 2012; etc.), the foreign press corps in China is heavily male dominated.[1] Although worldwide gender imbalance of journalism practitioners is improving (Hanitzsch & Hanusch, 2012; Gallagher, 2010), compared with decades ago when only 15% of London-based foreign correspondents were women in 1980s (Morrison & Tumber, 1985), the overall picture of 'male-as-norm and woman-as-interloper' (Byerly & Ross, 2006, p. 79) is still a harsh reality.

The situation is even worse for women journalists from non-Western countries, as women make up only 18.5% of the whole non-Western press corps operating in China. The largest number of China reporting corps by country, Japanese correspondents, according to the 'Foreign Press Directory 2015' issued by the International Information Office, are almost all men.

This striking gender imbalance of the China press corps is not unexpected. Assignment in China, though not as challenging as in war zones, is still widely considered tough, with its notoriously restrictive media culture and worrying pollution; meanwhile, overseas posting involves the cross-national or even cross-continental relocation of the whole family, and women journalists may sometimes be discouraged by traditional gender stereotypes. The only African correspondent, Aina Julietta of Nigeria Television, took the China correspondent position because her husband is working in China.[2]

Previous studies suggest that a correlation exists between newspeople's gender and news production (Armstrong, 2004; Craft & Wanta, 2004). Although it is not within the scope of this book to measure the potential impact of gender imbalance on foreign new production, women correspondents in this study do perceive a power difference in the field, and they cope with external pressures on their work differently than do men. When asked in the survey to rate their perceived influence from Chinese regulators and coercive harassment when reporting in China, women respondents report significantly stronger influence from these sources of disruptive pressure,[3] especially for coercive harassment.

Elite education and institutionalized cultural capital

Formal education is an indicator of social position. Elite education usually entails high cultural capital (i.e. knowledge), or specifically institutionalized cultural capital (Bourdieu, 1986), and social capital (i.e. social networks), which are two key career assets for journalists (Hummel, Kirchhoff & Prandner, 2012). Among foreign correspondents, a pattern of elite education is widely identified in previous studies (Van Ginneken, 1998; Wu & Hamilton, 2004), as this profession usually involves agents with high cultural and social capital, such as foreign language skills and social networks.

In the case of China correspondents, their collective primary habitus of elite education figures in prominence. Only three of the respondents have not attended formal college education; 45.5% of them have a master's degree, and seven out of the 101 respondents hold a doctoral degree. Decent formal education seems to be an indispensable attribute for a wannabe foreign correspondent, especially for those from Liberal countries, where all correspondents have a college degree or above, many of which were gained from elite universities such as Cambridge, Oxford, UC Berkley, Columbia, and Stanford. Take the *Financial Times* Beijing bureau. Bureau Chief Charles Clover went to Wisconsin-Madison and Johns Hopkins; Deputy Bureau Chief Lucy Hornby graduated from Princeton; Yuan Yang is a graduate from Oxford.

Some non-Western correspondents also obtained their degrees from elite American universities. Indian correspondent Ananth Krishnan holds a master's degree from the University of Chicago. But overall, non-Western and Polarized Pluralist countries impose slightly looser entry delimitation for China correspondents.

Chinese mind, Chinese habitus

A 'Chinese mind' is argued to be needed for fair reporting and understanding of China (Fu, 1990). This 'achieved' status (Lee, 1990) is bred through journalists' previous life experience connected to China, such as formal education on China (degrees in Chinese language or China/Asia studies) and personal connections with China (Chinese family upbringing, having close social connections in China, etc.). Such bred 'Chinese mind' is called in this book 'Chinese habitus.' The construct of Chinese habitus encompasses linguistic and cultural competencies of China (i.e. cognitive and conative dimensions) and an interest in China (affective dimension).

To dive deeper into the Chinese habitus of China correspondents, I identified some key quantifiable indicators of this construct and asked survey respondents to best provide answers to these variables. They include Chinese-language proficiency, formal education on China/Chinese, length of the China stint, and personal connection with China.[4] These four variables are

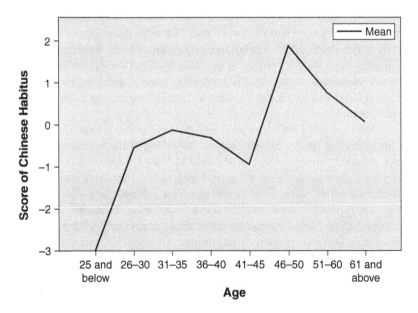

Figure 3.1 Chinese Habitus Score by Age Group

converted to their z-score respectively and computed into a new composite variable 'Chinese habitus.'[5]

China correspondents' Chinese habitus is found to vary significantly between different age groups.[6] Those in their late 40s on average score highest on Chinese habitus ($M = 1.88$, $SD = .68$), while young correspondents under 30 and those in their early 40s score lowest. The generational pattern is hard to be overlooked.

Take US journalists as an example. Bennett (1990) categorizes American correspondents to China into three waves: the first wave studied China from a distance in the 1960s and 1970s; the second wave are professional journalists assigned to China in the 1980s but knew very little about China; and the third wave, educated after China's opening-up, were elite and liberal, and had more hands-on experience and in-depth understanding on China, as they have easier and more diverse access to either formal or informal China education (Song and Lee, 2014). The third wave Anglo-American journalists, now in their 40s or early 50s, with outstanding Chinese habitus, have become the backbone of the foreign press corps in China.

Backbone generation

An exemplar of this backbone generation is Anthony Kuhn, NPR Beijing correspondent for four years. Born in the 1960s to the prestigious American sinologist Philip Kuhn and his Chinese wife Cheng Wu, Anthony Kuhn attended the China Studies graduate programme at Nanjing University in China. His Mandarin is good enough to make him an internet star in China.[7] BBC's China editor Gracie Carrie belongs to the same backbone gang. After graduating from Oxford, she was teaching English in China before joining BBC in the 1980s; Carrie is married to a Chinese national and is a fluent Chinese speaker herself. *New York Times* Beijing correspondent Chris Buckley earned his PhD in China Studies from China's Renmin University in the 1990s and had been working in China as a translator and teacher before becoming a China correspondent. His Chinese linguistic and cultural competencies are hailed by his peers as a model to look up to.[8] Canadian Ian Johnson, a Pulitzer Prize–winning journalist having covered China for *The New York Times* and *The Wall Street Journal*, the author of two books on China, studied Chinese in college in Florida and then Sinology for graduate programme in Berlin in the 1980s. He wrote his bachelor's degree thesis on foreign reporting in China, while he was on an exchange programme in Peking University as a senior colleague student. American journalist Mike Forsythe, best known for his investigative series on top Chinese leaders' hidden family wealth, studied Chinese at Tsinghua University in Beijing in the late 1990s and joined Bloomberg's Beijing office upon graduation.[9] The list goes on.

In the same age group, however, correspondents from continental Euro-pean countries (especially Democratic Corporatist countries in Hallin and Mancini's typology) are less equipped with such Chinese habitus, as most of them are on their first China stint, dispatched from home desks for a short and exotic overseas assignment before a promotion to a senior position at home. I would say that came to China with little preparation on 'Chineseness' and are not motivated to acquire much China-related cultural capital while on the job, as they know their position is secured for a three or four years' term. Take the Finnish public broadcaster YLE Beijing correspondent Mika Mäkeläinen. Without speaking any Chinese, Mäkeläinen had just freshly landed in his China posting when I met him in Beijing in late 2015, and less than two years later, while I am completing the book draft, he has already fin-ished his China stint and is headed back to the foreign news desk in Finland.[10]

New wave

The Chinese habitus of younger correspondents in their early 30s or late 20s is rather homogenous across all different home countries. Mostly born in the 1980s or 1990s and educated in a new global order in which China is growing to unprecedented prominence, they may well be labelled as the 'new wave.' Their encounter with China is largely facili-tated by the country's rapid economic development and, especially in the metropolis, the social networks and a growing number of Chinese mil-lennials who share more similarities with their Western peers compared with older generations. Many of them have worked or studied in China before embarking on China reporting. Matt Sheehan, a Stanford alum-nus in his late 20s, had already lived in China for three years when he got the job as the *HuffPost*'s first ever China correspondent in 2014. He speaks fluent Chinese and had taught, studied, and worked in China as an ordinary *Laowai* (foreigner); an international relations major, he runs his own blog and newsletter writing about China and Sino-US relations. As young journalists like Sheehan are mostly unestablished in journal-ism, their Chinese linguistic and cultural competencies understandably facilitate them entering the field.

A peculiarly outstanding trait of this new generation of China corre-spondents is the influx of ethnic Chinese. As Chinese laws forbid Chinese nationals from working as journalists for foreign media in China, the foreign press corps in China traditionally have a foreign face. Though a handful of resourceful Western media outlets try to keep several ethnic Chinese as staff journalists, a Chinese face has always been a rarity, and the very rare eth-nic Chinese journalists are usually second- or even third-generation descen-dants of immigrants.[11] Since the 1990s, with China's blistering economic development and deepened opening-up, there has been a soaring amount of emigration among Chinese family of higher socioeconomic status. The aftermath of Tiananmen bloodshed also contributed to an increase in the number of well-educated Chinese choosing to leave the country (Li, 2005). Especially Hong Kong's handover in 1997 prompted Hong Kong's large emigration to Canada and the UK. These new immigrants are more 'Chinese' than the second- or third-generation immigrants, knowing the language as native speakers and exhibiting adept understanding of Chinese culture and society. Thus we observe an evident increase of ethnic Chinese among the new wave of China correspondents, including Yuan Yang of *Financial Times*, Gerry Shih of Associated Press, Joanna Chiu of Agence France Presse, Didi Tang of the *London Times*, Steven Jiang of CNN, and Yang Xifan of German newspaper *Die Zeit*, just to name a few. Almost all of them were born in China (or Hong Kong) in the 1980s or 1970s and immigrated to the US, Canada, and the UK where they became foreign nationals.[12]

Take Joanna Chiu, Agence France Presse China and Mongolia correspondent. She was born in Hong Kong in the late 1980s and immigrated to Canada with her family after the Tiananmen crackdown in 1989. Growing up in Canada, Chiu went to the US to study journalism at Columbia University, after which she came back to Hong Kong and started her journalist career there. In a similar case, Gerry Shih was born in the US to two academic parents who migrated from Kunming, a city in southwest China; he speaks not only Mandarin Chinese, but also the dialect of Kunming.

In field reporting in a party-state like China, being ethnic Chinese helps journalists to blend into the local settings, making it easier to dodge unwanted attention and ensuing obstruction from local authorities. But it is not always a blessing to be ethnic Chinese reporting in China. There are situations in which interviewees are distrustful of fellow Chinese. In one episode of *SupChina*, a popular podcast for China watchers, Associated Press Greater China News Director Gillian Wong, a Singaporean Chinese, recounts how in Muslim-majority Xinjiang local Uygur were reluctant to talk to her because they thought she was Han Chinese – though this occurred against the larger background of antagonism between Han Chinese and Uygur that had flared up.[13]

Overall, Chinese habitus, including being ethnic Chinese, is an asset for entering the field of China correspondence, especially for young wannabe China correspondents who have very limited journalistic capital and habitus. Yet a distinct trajectory observed among young China correspondents is the path from freelancers to staff correspondents. Almost all, except for some working with news wires, landed in the current position after years of freelancing in the field. This pattern suggests Chinese habitus does not necessarily guarantee a competitive position. Journalistic habitus and capital other than Chinese knowledge are weighted more by most news organizations.

Chinese language

If ethnicity can sometimes be a double-edged sword, the asset of Chinese-language proficiency, as the conative dimension of Chinese habitus, is always highly valued for China correspondents. Major Anglo-American news organizations such as Reuters, *The New York Times*, and *The Wall Street Journal* set Chinese-language ability as an essential quality for new recruits.

Of the survey respondents, 40% speak fluent or above Chinese (8% are native Chinese speakers); 29% speak intermediate Chinese, while another 24% say they only speak basic Chinese. Seven percent of them do not speak any Chinese. As in actual interviews or research, 'intermediate' proficiency is barely conducive, we can say that a majority of China correspondents (60%) do not have sufficient Chinese proficiency. Although the measurement only reflects correspondents' self-evaluation of their Chinese proficiency, the overall picture tells that Chinese language is not an essential entry threshold in the field of China correspondence.

The aforementioned Ian Johnson, a fluent Chinese speaker himself, is an ardent believer in the essentiality of knowing the local language for foreign reporting. In an article reflecting on his decades' experience of learning Chinese, he wrote,

> foreign reporting was wanting in part because of the inability of most foreign correspondents to speak the local language . . . how could you do anything worthwhile without knowing the language? It's the only way to get close to people, know their thoughts, recreate internal dialogue.[14]

Peruvian journalist Isolda Morillo is one of the very few, if not the only, foreign correspondents in China who write and publish literature in Chinese. Her parents, both university professors, moved to China to teach literature since the 1980s, giving young Morillo her first contact with China. Such experiences bred, in her own words, her 'strong Chinese complex,' an avid interest in China's society and culture which shaped her thirst to learn the language. She mainly taught herself and entered the field of China reporting, first as a journalist for Spanish Television and then for the Associated Press of the United States.

Language inability frustrates foreign correspondents and impairs their work, as they have to rely on translators and local assistants, who in effect function as the correspondents' 'gatekeeper,' undermining their autonomy in work. Colombian correspondent Santiago Villa speaks little Chinese. He is frank about his deep anxiety over the language inability:

> It's very limiting to do reporting without knowing Chinese; you just scratch the surface . . . when you use a translator for interview, you don't get to know the full narratives . . . you don't get to have a dialogue with the interviewee. Usually the meaning of your question gets lost in translation.[15]

But institutionally, for many foreign correspondents, especially for those from Democratic Corporatist and Polarized Pluralist countries, language inability does not prevent them from getting the job, as after all, it is still very challenging for news organizations to recruit talents with both language skills and journalistic literacy. Most news outlets in these countries do not offer incentive or impose any requirement for their correspondents to learn Chinese. Learning Chinese on the job is more a self-initiated challenge. Some interviewees are taking Chinese courses at their own expense in their spare time, but 'it's very difficult to hang on there,' as German correspondent Steffen Wurzel admits.[16]

Professional training and role perceptions: journalistic habitus

Journalistic professional norms and values such as immediacy, objectivity, and public service shape journalists' position and practice in the field, more than do personal idiosyncrasies (see e.g. Benson & Hallin, 2007; Deuze, 2005; Donsbach, 2009; Esser, 2008; Hovden, 2008; Shoemaker & Reese, 1996, 2013). These professional norms and values, usually packaged as 'journalistic ideology,' 'a system of beliefs characteristic of professional journalism' (Deuze, 2005, p. 445), can be understood as the cognitive and conative dimensions of journalistic habitus.[17] It functions to self-legitimize journalists' position in the field and broader social space (Deuze, 2005; Schudson, 2001; Zelizer, 2004).

Unlike Chinese habitus, measuring journalistic habitus on a point-based scale would be problematic, as the specific content of the required expertise and values of the profession in different media systems, though seen as convergent with the Anglo-American liberal journalism tradition, still diverge in various forms (see, for example, Hanitzsch et al., 2011; Voltmer, 2012; Zeng, 2018). Yet journalistic ideology is widely argued to foster and maintain a professional consensus and recognition among journalists (see, for example, Deuze, 2005; Schudson and Anderson, 2009), although the social base and the specific value of the ideology differ across countries and media systems. Journalistic norms and values such as objectivity and the 'gut' (Schultz, 2007) judgment of newsworthiness are institutionally defined, explicitly taught both through formal education and through on-the-job learning in newsroom practices (Tumber & Prentoulis, 2005). Values and perceptions of the profession fall into the cognitive dimension of journalistic habitus, best to be embodied in journalistic role perception. Therefore, in the following session I only discuss the professional training and role perception of China correspondents as two indicators of their journalistic habitus.

Professional training

Pedelty (1995) found among foreign correspondents in El Salvador that those 'trained in fields other than journalism' tended to produce more in-depth, critical reporting. Van Ginneken (1998) notes that 'journalistic ideology' bred in professional journalism training guides journalists towards routine frames. The former *HuffPost* China correspondent Matt Sheehan, who had no journalistic training before taking up the job at the *HuffPost*, describes such journalistic habitus as baggage: 'If you arrive in China as a journalist, without really knowing the country yet, everything you see is organized in a story pattern, with a good guy and a bad guy, and certainly with a conclusion.'[18]

Foreign correspondents traditionally are not prominently identified by formal journalism education. Tunstall (1974) characterizes many British foreign correspondents as the product of Oxford or Cambridge in fields other than journalism; Willnat and Weaver (2003) note that only 34% of US-based foreign correspondents have a university degree in journalism; Harding (1990) and Bennett (1990) recount that some of the US journalists in China who did not major in journalism or Chinese studies ranked among the most distinguished performers. A similar pattern is also identified among present-day China correspondents. Overall, only one-third of the respondents have received formal journalism education at a college or graduate school, as Table 3.1 shows; the ratio is even lower for non-Western correspondents: only 25.9% (N = 7) of them have had formal journalism education. They are mostly trained in other related fields of political sciences, international relations, history, economics, and China or Asia studies.

Yet, in America where journalistic professionalism is stronger, formal education in journalism does appear to be a more important quality to enter the field. Many correspondents from US news organizations hold a degree in journalism from elite universities. *New York Times* former

Beijing bureau chief Edward Wong gained his master's degree in journalism from UC Berkley, and Rob Schmitz, Shanghai correspondent for NPR, has a master's degree in journalism from Columbia University. In contrast, the only African correspondent, Aina Julietta of Nigerian National TV, majored in French. Indian correspondent Ananth Krishnan of *India Today* holds a master's degree in Indian history. Sutirtho Patranobis, another Indian correspondent for the *Hindustan Times*, majored in English literature.

Even when they are in the field, the elite professional education continues to be entrenched through fellowships for further journalism training and teaching journalism in education institutions, thus reproducing the existing structure of covering China. *New York Times*' Edward Wong briefly joined the journalism faculty at Princeton University teaching international reporting after an eight-year China stint; Julie Makinen, former China bureau chief of the *Los Angeles Times*, is on a one-year John S. Knight Journalism Fellowship at Stanford University at the time of this writing. Though the linkage between journalism as a profession and journalism education is to be found in many other countries, it comes in its strongest form in the setting of Anglo-American countries, echoing the strong professionalism in the liberal media system.

On-the-job training in the newsroom is another crucial venue for breeding journalistic norms and values. I'll discuss this aspect in Chapter 4 on organizational-level dynamics in the field.

Journalistic role perceptions

Journalistic role perceptions spread across a spectrum, from detached neutral reporting adhering to objectivity to a more critical advocacy journalism. This cognitive dimension of journalistic habitus is shaped by professional training and media culture, among others. It entails the beliefs and values China correspondents uphold in their profession and its social functions, with an immediate bearing on their journalistic practice.

Scholars have outlined three traditions of journalistic role: public service tradition of objective and neutral reporting, advocacy tradition emphasizing the political role of journalists pursuing partisan goals, and market tradition with strong audience orientation (see e.g. Donsbach, 2009). Hanitzsch (2007) further identifies three measureable dimensions: interventionism, power distance, and market orientation. Journalistic interventionism reflects 'the extent to which journalists pursue a particular mission and promote certain values' (Hanitzsch, 2007, p. 372). Any role typology between 'neutral disseminator,' 'gatekeeper' and 'participant,' and 'advocate' falls into this dimension. At the passive end of the spectrum, which emphasizes objectivity, neutrality, detachment, and impartiality, journalists see themselves as detached and uninvolved transmitters of information only. The other end of the spectrum denotes 'the active support of particular values, positions, groups and social change' (Hanitzsch et al., 2011, p. 280).

Power distance, addressing the journalists' position toward the external political or economic power, stretches from 'adversary' (high power distance) to 'loyal' (low power distance). The adversarial approach echoes the notion of the 'Fourth Estate' and the critical watchdog in the Anglo-American journalism tradition. 'Loyal' journalists with low power distance take on a propagandist role, defending those in power and serving as a mouthpiece of the government or the party. The official requirement for journalists to be 'absolutely loyal' to the Party in China exemplifies the negative end in this dimension.

The dimension of market orientation ranges from the most market-oriented journalism with a strong emphasis on profit to the least market-oriented public or civic journalism. Market-oriented journalists focus on what the audiences want to know, rather than what they need to know, and are highly driven by consumerism and audience ratings, whereas citizenry-oriented journalists see themselves as key agents for an informed citizenry and hold the public interest as their priority.

Borrowing from Hanitzsch's (2011) interview design covering the three dimensions of journalistic role perceptions,[19] I compiled a block of questions on role perception, including 11 statements in the survey, and invited respondents to note their agreement on each statement on a five-point scale (1 being least important, 5 being extremely important).

A comparison of the mean score of each item across the four media systems (Table 3.2) pictures an overall audience-oriented and objectivity-upheld foreign press corps who rated 'provide home audience with accurate and objective knowledge about China' and 'provide home audience with the most interesting information' with the highest score. A general tendency toward detachment is also prominent. Thus, in the field of China correspondence, some journalistic values appear to be universal: pursuing detached, independent journalism with an emphasis on objectivity and the audience. China correspondents as a whole are not interested in cultivating citizenry in China, as they scored uniformly low on the item 'motivating citizens in China to participate in civic activity and political discussion'; nor are they interested in 'supporting Chinese official policies,' indicating a uniformly high distance from the power centre of the host country.

Meanwhile, they vary noticeably in the monitorial role of serving as a watchdog ('act as watchdog of Chinese government/business elites in China'), an advocacy role for social change in China, and a loyal role to home government with low power distance ('support home country official

Table 3.2 Role Perception across Countries

	Mean (SD)	Liberal	Democratic Corporatist	Polarized Pluralist	Non-Western
Provide home audience with accurate and objective knowledge about China	4.59*** (.59)	4.83 (.38)	4.60 (.50)	4.78 (.43)	4.15 (.72)
Provide home audience with the information that is most interesting	4.10 (.83)	4.17 (.81)	4.30 (.57)	4.17 (.86)	3.82 (.96)
Be an absolutely detached China observer	3.51 (1.14)	3.33 (1.22)	3.65 (.93)	3.78 (1.22)	3.44 (1.12)
Provide home citizens with information they need to make political decisions related to China	3.07 (1.16)	3.36 (1.07)	2.90 (.97)	2.61 (1.38)	3.11 (1.19)
Act as a watchdog of the Chinese government	2.62** (1.22)	3.08 (1.27)	2.35 (1.04)	2.78 (1.11)	2.11 (1.15)
Act as a watchdog of the business elites in China	2.50** (1.10)	2.89 (1.14)	2.40 (.99)	2.72 (1.07)	1.89 (.89)
Influence public opinion about China	2.45 (1.21)	2.58 (1.32)	2.20 (1.15)	2.22 (.88)	2.59 (1.31)
Advocate or help to advocate for social change in China	1.96* (1.10)	2.11 (1.14)	1.45 (.69)	2.50 (1.25)	1.78 (1.01)
Motivate citizens in China to participate in civic activity and political discussion	1.69 (.94)	1.83 (.97)	1.60 (1.05)	1.67 (.84)	1.59 (.89)
Support Chinese official policies to bring about prosperity and development	1.47 (.81)	1.31 (.75)	1.30 (.73)	1.61 (.85)	1.70 (.87)
Support home country official foreign policy with China	1.59*** (.99)	1.28 (.74)	1.60 (.99)	1.22 (.55)	2.26 (1.20)
N	101	36	20	18	27

* $p < .05$
** $p < .01$
*** $p < .001$

foreign policy with China'), though the overall scores for the latter two items are considerably low.

Correspondents from liberal countries clearly demonstrate a higher degree of identification with the monitorial role than do their counterparts from non-Western countries,[20] in line with the watchdog tradition in these countries. In addition, China's restrictive regulations and tight press censorship can work to provoke correspondents from the liberal media system to play a strong watchdog role over Chinese political and business power or to take the watchdog role on behalf of their Chinese peers. As French (2014) notes, for China correspondents, 'breaking stories that the censored Chinese press can't touch has long been a core part of the mission.' The 2012–2013 wave of investigative reports on China's high-level officials' corruption,[21] and the 2017–2018 wave of impactful stories revealing China's secret crackdown on Muslims in its Muslim-majority autonomous region Xinjiang,[22] are all led by US news organizations. Of course, it's worth pointing out that these investigative reports are possible also because the news organizations are the most resourceful ones.

Advocacy orientation is overall weak[23] but clearly stronger among correspondents from Polarized Pluralist countries ('advocate or help to advocate social change in China,' $M = 2.5$), namely, France, Spain, and Italy. Following the strong advocacy journalism tradition in these countries (Hallin & Mancini, 2004), correspondents are more likely to engage in advocating for social change in China. In December 2015, China refused to renew the visa of French correspondent Ursula Gauthier, thus effectively expelling the journalist, for an opinionated article she wrote critical of Chinese policy toward the ethnic minorities in Xinjiang. This 'opinion journalism' tradition in French media culture (Chalaby, 1996; Kuhn, 1995) is different from the Anglo-American tradition of a 'Chinese wall' between facts and opinion. It is clearly even less welcomed in China where unorthodox opinion is never truly allowed.

A mixed picture of China correspondents' role perceptions unfolds here: they universally accept the basic values of liberal journalistic professionalism such as objectivity, neutrality, and detachment; the majority holds a non-facilitative, non-advocate approach with very high power distance when covering China, in line with a typical liberal journalistic professionalism. However, the broader picture of role perception among China correspondents still diverges in key dimensions, including a watchdog role for the host country, advocacy orientation, and power distance with the home government.

Non-Western correspondents from less independent journalistic cultures show a stronger alignment with political power and less interest in a monitorial or interventionist role.[24] A majority of non-Western countries in this study (Russia, Singapore, Japan, South Korea, India, etc.), though many are identified as 'hybrid' in terms of media systems and journalistic cultures (Voltmer, 2012), share some similarities in high clientelism, weak journalistic professionalism, and strong state intervention (Vartanova, 2012; Voltmer, 2008), which explains the less independent journalistic culture where correspondents generally show weak identification with a monitorial role and strong collaboration with political power.

Elsewhere (Zeng, 2018), I categorized the present-day China correspondents into *detached disseminator*, *populist watchdog*, and *facilitative change agent*, according to their varying role perceptions along the three dimensions. More than one-third are categorized as the least intervention-ist 'detached disseminator,' with the strongest emphasis on objectivity and neutral reporting; nearly half of China correspondents fall into the cluster of 'popular watchdog,' characterized with stronger audience orientation and monitorial approach; only a very small number of China correspon-dents are identified as 'facilitative change agent,' driven by the strongest interventionism impetus and facilitative approach to cooperate with the official tone of their home government. The last type is most likely to face Chinese accusation of the foreign media being 'hostile foreign forces with an agenda.'

Spiralists, Sinophiles, Sinojournos, and Sporadics: a habitus-based typology

As repeatedly emphasized throughout this book, the variance in foreign cor-respondents' habitus is closely related to their positions in the field. Hannerz (2004) categorizes China correspondents into three types: *Spiralists* who come for a certain length of stint and leave for the next posting afterwards, *Sinophiles* whose priority *is* China rather than to *report* on China and who were barely based elsewhere as a journalist, and national journalists spo-radically on one overseas stint (I call them *Sporadics*). The typology helps to identify how individual agents are positioned differently with different habitus in the field of China correspondence.

However, Hannerz's typology does not cover all patterns for present-day China correspondents. Besides *Sinophiles*, there is another group who tries to balance both China and journalism as their priorities. They are different from *Sinophiles* mainly in their *affective dimension* of journalistic habitus, or the desire and commitment they invest into the journalistic field. Unlike Sinophiles who hold rather weak affection in journalism and practice it only as a conduit for their strong affection in other China-related fields (aca-demia, foreign policy, or public relations), this fourth category are heavily committed to both China and journalism; they stay in China for a consider-ably long time to cover China as professional journalists. For convenience of discussion, I call them *Sinojournos*.

One can thus observe four types of journalists in the field of China corre-spondence: *Spiralists*, *Sporadics*, *Sinophiles*, and *Sinojournos*, with distinc-tively varying habitus. They represent four types of positions in the field, unavoidably resulting in different strategies and practices.

For a clear empirical picture of this typology, I used a two-step clustering analysis to group the survey respondents based on their *Chinese* habitus, number of previous overseas postings, and years of working as a China correspondent.[25] As discussed earlier, *Sinophiles* and *Sinojournos* should score the highest in Chinese habitus, but *Sinojournos* have much more experience working as a China correspondent; *Spiralists* are the most experienced in previous overseas assignments, while *Sporadics* do not excel in either Chinese habitus or foreign correspondent experience.[26]

The majority of China correspondents are *Sinophiles* (43.6%) and *Sporadics* (35.6%), both of whom do not have much foreign reporting experience; 10.9% of the respondents are *Spiralists*, or professional foreign correspondents, for whom a China posting is only one passing chapter in their excitement-ridden journey of foreign reporting around the globe. They did not have much China-related socialization before being posted to China, scoring lowest in Chinese habitus. An even smaller proportion is categorized as the most committed *Sinojournos*, who score highest in Chinese habitus and have stayed in China as foreign correspondents for most, if not all, of their professional lives.

An overseas assignment for most news outlets runs between three and five years. Both *Spiralists* and *Sporadics* stay in China for barely one term, and *Sinophiles* on average stay for one to two terms. Although most *Sinophiles* and *Sinojournos* try to stay on longer after their term is done,[27] most news organizations expect their foreign correspondents to return to the home desk or switch bureaus. The rationale behind such common practice of news organizations, as explained by Morrison and Tumber (1985), is that staying on an overseas posting too long may make the correspondents 'go native' (p. 461), meaning upholding too strong local habitus, which is argued to blind the fresh eye of correspondents when reporting the over-familiar host country. Similarly, familiarity with Chinese society and the language structurally facilitates understanding cultural messages, but it also breeds inattention to occurrences. Thus, most news organizations set limits on each overseas posting to keep their foreign correspondents 'fresh.'

Table 3.3 Cluster Analysis Result of China Correspondents' Career Pattern

types	N (%)	Chinese habitus M (SD)	Number of previous overseas postings M (SD)	Years of working as China correspondent M (SD)
Spiralists	11 (10.9)	−2.68 (.90)	3.00 (1.10)	3.27 (2.51)
Sporadics	36 (35.6)	−2.07 (1.01)	.42 (.50)	2.74 (1.78)
Sinophiles	44 (43.6)	1.32 (1.27)	.32 (.52)	6.65 (3.81)
Sinojournos	10 (9.9)	4.58 (1.42)	.70 (.67)	20.05 (4.86)
Total	101			

However, an increasing number of news organizations now tend to be flexible with the contract length if the correspondent exhibits strong Chinese habitus to minimize the organizational cost of training a new replacement. This is especially common with Anglo-American news organizations who have been in effect setting the international news agenda. A senior editor at Reuters said they encourage correspondents to stay longer because 'Even if you are an experienced journalist (and) you speak Chinese, it takes at least a year to figure out what's going on.'[28]

Spiralists: globetrotting news hotspots

Spiralists make foreign correspondence their career but are not confined to one specific posting. They cover different transitional and volatile regions in the world, moving between stints which normally range from three to five years. They are thus most likely to possess 'cosmopolitan' habitus (Hannerz, 2004). Jane Perlez of *The New York Times* in Beijing is one of such typical cosmopolitan Spiralists. She covered the Afghan war, the famine in Somalia, the civil wars in Sudan and Somalia, and gold mining in Southeast Asia before joining the *Times* Beijing office. Bernhand Zand of *Der Spiegel* has been based in Istanbul, Cairo, and Dubai covering wars and conflicts before coming to China in 2012. Spanish correspondent Javier Espinosa of *El Mundo* spent 12 years reporting from the conflict-stricken Middle East before trying his hand in China since 2014.

To a certain extent, they are *international correspondents* rather than *foreign correspondents*. This is especially true for those working with international media such as Reuters, Agence France Presse, and CNN. A Beijing-based Reuters correspondent objects to being labelled as 'foreign correspondents': 'We are not *foreign correspondents*. At Reuters we only have *correspondents*. No country is "foreign" to us.' Yet such 'stateless' quality is only ideal. 'Cosmopolitan' international correspondents still carry baggage from home, from the social system and education system they came from. As Hannerz (2007) admits, 'any claim to cosmopolitanism would seem to be weakened' (p. 307).

Although lacking local knowledge and connections, they are seen as contributing to the field of China correspondence with the strongest journalistic habitus, especially in the *affective dimension*. 'The best job in the world' is what I heard most from Spiralists on how they like their job as a foreign correspondent.

Having been posted in a number of other global news hotspots, they tend to believe that their professional perception and practice are well applied in the different social settings they cover. Thus, this group of China correspondents would transfer their doxic practice in the journalistic fields in other national contexts directly into that of China, in many cases, challenging the power relations with institutional constraints. How *Der Spiegel* Beijing correspondent Bernhand Zand compares his China assignment to his previous postings is representative:

> I interviewed, in Middle East, heads of the states, from the king of Jordan, president of Syria, to the prince of Dubai, the president of Turkey, etc. All these people spoke relatively freely to us. . . . But [in China] I don't know why they [Chinese leaders] are so shy to speak to western press.[29]

Spiralists' challenges to the status quo of the field may come with real impact. A *Sinojourno* himself, Chris Buckley notes that *Spiralists*, by daring to 'do stories that would offend the government, knowing that they are only staying for a short time,'[30] create pressure on the whole foreign press corps to stay alert and sensitive to topics which they might otherwise overlook or self-censor.

Sinojournos: lifetime commitment in both China and journalism

Sinojournos tend to stay for a considerable length in China, in some cases for their entire professional life, strongly committed to China or the greater China area. They are affectively devoted to reporting China, regarding China as 'one of the wonderful places to be for a reporter, because it is both amazing and important.'[31] Sinojournos are mostly found in Anglo-American media organizations.

Veteran China correspondent Jaime FlorCruz, who has spent more than 40 years living and working in China, was a student at Peking University in the 1970s before he started working as a news assistant with *Time* magazine, which led to this lifelong profession as a China correspondent. Chris Buckley started as a researcher for the *New York Times* Beijing office before becoming a professional journalist with Reuters for seven years and then with *The New York Times* again. Both have spent their entire careers in China and are established as exemplary China correspondents, highly respected for their resourceful local connections and unbeatable knowledge of the host country.

Possessing this vital cultural and social capital, Sinojournos are most likely to become star journalists – journalists with huge symbolic capital, which transforms into more social and even economic capital, thus further consolidating their already advantageous position in the field. As one example of Sinojournos' outstanding social and symbolic capital in China reporting, they are known for being able to maintain good relationships with high-ranking Chinese officials. Former MOFA spokeswoman Jiang Yu is said to habitually only address Jaime FlorCruz and Chris Buckley by their first names in formal press conferences, which is rare in China.[32] This accumulated capital breeds inertia, keeping Sinojournos in the field of China correspondence even longer. With extensive local connections and rich knowledge about China, they often become the reference group among the foreign press corps, for sources, story frames, etc.

Sinophiles: give me China. I don't care much about journalism

Sinophiles, although highly committed to Chineseness, hold very weak *affection* for the field of journalism. They do not desire to play the game of journalism. Usually they aim at a career as *China experts* or *Sinologists*, rather than *China correspondents*. They may serve a very short stint as a professional journalist in China, followed by other professions outside journalism, in either academia or business. Whichever non-journalistic profession they switch to, the focus is always on China; the job as a China correspondent offers them a means to stay in China as well as to establish Chinese connections.

HuffPost's Matt Sheehan, having lived in China for five years with a keen interest in Sino-US relations and Chinese culture, left the China correspondent job only after two years. When asked why the retreat, Sheehan said, 'Well, it's interesting, but not a sustainable career.' Now, he joined a US think tank on China policy and meanwhile runs his blog and newsletter on Sino-US relations.

Isolda Morillo, the Associate Press journalist that I mentioned earlier, recently left her job as a journalist for family reasons, after being a China correspondent for more than a decade. She says that she will not be practicing the profession in other parts of the world. 'I will only practice journalism in China. . . . Practicing journalism for me is doing field research, which is the best way to understand China.' When asked how she would identify herself, Morillo used the term 'empirical Sinologist': 'Between "China studies" and China reporting, I chose the latter; I don't want to be a Sinologist in the Ivory Tower. My research and studies are my field research, i.e., the stories I filed.' She is now running a publishing company, to pursue her passion in Chinese literature.

Other Sinophiles can be even more detached from the trade of journalism. A Turkish journalist has been in China for more than a decade. He helped set up the China bureaus for a number of Turkish media, including its national news agency and for national TV. At the time of my fieldwork in Beijing, he served as the China correspondent for the Turkish national newspaper *Yurt*, but was planning to retreat from journalism. 'The income is very bad (practicing journalism),' he reflects on the profession as a China correspondent. But it was a reporting trip to Japan that made him determined to leave journalism. Sent to neighbouring Japan to cover the devastating earthquake in 2011, he realized upon arrival that the situation was life-threatening. He asked to leave the site, but his employer insisted that he fly to the epicentre and report from there. Frustrated, he chose to sneak away with a rescue team from Australia. 'I can still write something about China if the Turkish embassy or whoever approaches me for stories. But now I'm mainly engaged in film making,' he concludes with relief and satisfaction.

Sinophiles usually do not try to challenge the existing power relations in the field. Instead, they mostly follow the norms in the safest way and interact less with peer correspondents. To them, journalism is just a means for gaining 'Chineseness' or even just for living, sometimes a transition to other more lucrative fields, i.e., where they can more easily gain capital in various forms.

Sporadics: journalism at home; China just a passing interest

Unlike Spiralists, Sporadics do not take foreign correspondence as their lifetime profession. They exhibit very limited affection for the game of foreign correspondence and weak *Chinese* habitus. They have long been journalists at home desks and are brought to China by some sporadic assignments. Most of them do not have plans to stay in China for long, and, in most cases, expect to return home after the China stint, ideally with a promotion. To many of them, the China assignment, apart from its innate attractiveness, serves as a stepping stone.

Sporadics are mostly seen among correspondents from non-Western and continental European countries. Most Japanese journalists work in the Beijing bureau or Shanghai bureau of their news organizations for one or two terms before returning, in some cases, as senior editorial writers (論説委員). German public radio ARD's Shanghai correspondent Steffen Wurzel began his China assignment in 2013, first as a summer replacement for the then Shanghai correspondent for several months, which led to a five-year China stint. His predecessor, after five years in China, went back to Berlin to open a café, never in journalism again. His colleague in the ARD Beijing office had just started his China posting (his first overseas assignment) when we met in early 2016, after more than 10 years reporting in Germany. Finnish public broadcaster YLE Beijing correspondent Mika Mäkeläinen, a veteran journalist with more than 20 years' experience in his home country of Finland, was serving a two-year China stint, which is, according to him, a 'company norm.'

Sporadics, exhibiting very limited Chinese habitus, more resemble what Hannerz (2004) distinguishes as 'expatriates.' They do not have strong commitment to the host country and its culture, often enjoying a lifestyle close to home. A German correspondent based in Shanghai told me he chooses to bring everything from Germany to China – from olive oil to flour – and lives in the heart of the old French Concession – a life nothing but European. In contrast, a typical Sinophile or Sinojourno is most likely to be found in a typical *hutong* (small and historical alley in an old residential area of Beijing) house and indulging himself or herself in street food.

This 'expatriate' positioning of Sporadics colours their way of journalistic practice in the field of China correspondence. They tend to rely more on press review and local hires (Chinese news assistants) instead of investing time to develop local connections, thus accumulating very limited cultural and social capital, which in turn effectively reinforces the existing structures in the field. Compared with the other three types of correspondents, especially Spiralists, expatriate Sporadics are also more attuned to organizational norms and control of their home countries.

Conclusion

This chapter looks into the habitus of China correspondents as the starting point for further scrutiny on the dynamics and structure of the field of China reporting. China correspondents come from a not-so-diverse demographic background in terms of education level and social class, yet they carry various professional beliefs and values, or journalistic habitus, and varying degree of Chinese habitus. Habitus and capital, together with organizational policy, distinguish China correspondents into four types: *Spiralists*, *Sporadics*, *Sinojournos*, and *Sinophiles*. These different positions further shape various sets of habitus, which are structured in journalists' own histories prior to their China posting, and also structure their positions in the field as well as the structures of the field.

I focussed on the journalistic professional education and role perception as a window to China correspondents' journalistic habitus. A clear convergence towards detached, independent journalism with an emphasis on objectivity and the audience figures among China correspondents regardless of national contexts. But variance across media systems is evidenced in key dimensions, including a watchdog role for the host country, advocacy orientation and power distance with the home government, largely consistent with the respective journalistic culture in each media system, suggesting that the national journalistic culture still has a strong grip in foreign correspondence. These various role perceptions, as a major component of journalistic habitus, engage China correspondents in different power relations with the restrictive host regulations and cultures.

The formation of journalistic habitus, especially the cognitive dimension, is not only to be examined from the institutional level (institutionalized education and newsroom training) and societal level (media culture). Family upbringing also has a bearing on journalists' habitus and practices. This book does not particularly look into this factor, but some prominent examples are worth mentioning. Australian journalist John Garnaut, who became the centre of the current public concern and debate over Chinese influence in Australia, is one of them. The son to a renowned economist who served as the senior advisor to Australia's ambassador to China, Garnaut spent two years of his childhood in the Australian embassy in Beijing with his family. He worked as a China correspondent for eight years since 2007 before turning away from journalism and joining politics as the senior advisor to then Prime Minister Malcolm Turnbull.[33] In the heated public concern over 'Chinese influence' in Australia, Garnaut became a vocal voice, after being tasked to lead a secret investigation on Chinese influence in Australia, which directly led to the ensuing massive 'foreign interference law' revision. He was called one of 'the leaders of the recent anti-China panic in the Australian media' by former Labour Foreign Minister Bob Carr.[34]

Habitus sets the basis of power relations in the field of foreign correspondence. But as much as Bourdieu is not a determinist, I am by no means suggesting that habitus has the ominous power to structure or determine if an agent is to play a role of *Sinojourno*, *Spiralist*, *Sinophile*, or *Sporadic*. Habitus, especially journalistic and Chinese habitus, does play a major role in setting an agent's position and shaping her/his practice in the field of China correspondence, yet it is always in a fluid state, shaped and accumulated during the ever-stretching personal and social trajectory. The structuring of the position and field is a dynamic process, forever developing and evolving.

In addition to habitus, other factors including newsroom norms or routines, organizational constraints, and institutional pressure all contribute to the structure of the field of China correspondence and the position and practice of correspondents. The power of these factors and China correspondents' negotiation of their autonomy with these factors are discussed in the following chapters.

Notes

1 Other studies report a percentage of women journalists at around 30% to 40%.
2 Personal communication, November 2015.
3 One-Way ANOVA result: $F(1,98) = 4.550$, $p = .035$, $\eta^2 = .044$ for 'Chinese regulators,' $F(1,98) = 15.606$, $p = .000$, $\eta^2 = .137$ for 'coercive harassment.'

4 In the questionnaire, seven scenarios were provided for respondents to choose from to indicate the closest to their personal connection with China: (1) Born a Chinese national; (2) Ethnic Chinese or with Chinese origin; (3) Married to a Chinese; (4) In a relationship with a Chinese; (5) Having lived in China before China correspondent posting; (6) Other personal connections; (7) No personal connection with China. For easier computing in the composite variable 'Chinese habitus,' the original variable 'personal Chinese connection' was then recoded to indicate various depth of personal Chinese connection: (0) No personal connection with China; (1) Weak personal connection with China; (2) Strong personal connection with China (as in, e.g. 'born a Chinese national').

5 The internal reliability of these four variables is unsurprisingly only moderate (α = .52), as they are not necessarily interrelated. Instead, sometimes they are complementary to each other. Personal China-related life experience can be totally different from formal education in China studies or alike, which can be acquired outside of China. For example, a journalist may know China and Chinese language quite well because of personal China-related experience rather than formal education.

6 $F(7,63) = 3.59, p = .003$

7 Kuhn impressed the Chinese public for asking questions in fluent Chinese at a state press conference. See www.npr.org/sections/parallels/2017/03/18/519216823/for-years-ive-been-a-correspondent-in-china-this-month-i-became-a-viral-star

8 One of the survey/interview questions asks respondents to name one China correspondent whom they think is the best; many of them named Chris Buckley and cited 'his rich knowledge about China.'

9 Forsythe later joined the *New York Times* in 2013, after a sensational censorship scandal of Bloomberg.

10 Mäkeläinen explains to me it's a company policy, though he personally thinks two years' term is too short, especially for a China posting.

11 Melinda Liu of *Newsweek*, for example, is one of the very few ethnic Chinese journalists in the older generation of China correspondents.

12 Besides Chinese migrants in Anglophone countries, Chinese-majority city-state Singapore is another major source of such talents for China correspondence.

13 An audio file of the programme can be found here: http://supchina.com/podcasts/gillian-wong-josh-chin-journalism-careers-china/?platform=hootsuite

14 Johnson, I. (2018). China watching: language wars, from Montreal to Beijing. Retrieved from http://chinaheritage.net/journal/china-watching-language-wars-from-montreal-to-beijing/

15 Personal communication, February, 2016.

16 Personal communication, March, 2016.

17 Schultz (2007) defines journalistic habitus as 'a bodily knowledge and feel for the daily news game which can be seen in the journalistic practices surrounding qualification and legitimisation of newsworthiness' (p. 202).

18 Personal communication, August, 2017.

19 With slight modification to situate the questionnaire in the setting of foreign correspondence in China.

20 Correspondents from Liberal countries score $M = 3.08$ for 'watchdog of Chinese government' and $M = 2.89$ for 'watchdog for business elites in China'; correspondents from non-Western countries score $M = 2.11$ for 'watchdog of Chinese government' and $M = 1.89$ for 'watchdog for business elites in China.'

21 Reports include the *Wall Street Journal*'s story on the Bo Xilai scandal, the *New York Times*' investigation on then-Premier Wen Jiabao and top business

tycoon Wang Jianlin, as well as Bloomberg's story on the wealth of Xi Jinping's family.

22 Representative stories are from Gerry Shih of Associated Press, Megha Rajago-palan of BuzzFeed, Emily Rauhala of *The Washington Post*, and Josh Chin of *The Wall Street Journal*.

23 Correspondents from Democratic Corporatist countries show the least interest in this regard (M = 1.45).

24 Non-Western correspondents are more likely to stay loyal to the political power of their home government (M = 2.26) compared with their Western counterparts.

25 The affective dimension as subjective commitment is less direct to operational-ize. Before discussing its difference among the four types of China correspon-dents qualitatively, I use the length of China posting as an indicator for foreign journalists' desire in the field. The cognitive and conative dimensions of journal-istic habitus are not used as categorizing variables, for the reasons cited earlier.

26 The cluster result is satisfactory, with an average silhouette at 0.6, and all three variables score a larger than 0.65 predictor importance.

27 In such a scenario, correspondents usually can negotiate with their news com-panies for another term. But if the company policy is not as flexible, the cor-respondent would have to quit their job in order to stay on in China. An example is Australian ABC's Beijing correspondent Stephan McDonald. After his two terms with ABC was done, he left ABC to join BBC in order to stay on in China.

28 Personal communication, November, 2015.

29 Personal communication, January, 2016.

30 Personal communication, March, 2017.

31 Personal communication, January, 2016.

32 Personal communication, January 2016.

33 Lewis, C. (May 31, 2018). Meet the man at the heart of the latest Chinese influ-ence scandal. *Crikey*. Retrieved from https://www.crikey.com.au/2018/05/31/john-garnaut-just-who-is-the-man-at-the-centre-of-the-latest-china-contro versy/

34 McKenzie, N. & O'Malley, N. (May 28, 2018). Bob Carr enlists Labor in new China influence row. *The Sydney Morning Herald*. Retrieved from https://www.smh.com.au/politics/federal/bob-carr-enlists-labor-in-new-china-influence-row-20180528-p4zi0z.html

4 Organizational control and autonomy
Journalistic logic in the newsroom

Although foreign correspondents are the focal point of this book, they are not loners in foreign reporting or as heroic, freewheeling, and aloof from the bureaucratic hassles from the home desk as they may appear to be in the myth of foreign correspondents (Murrell, 2014). They are employees of news organizations, registered members of the 'tribe' of foreign press corps in the same host country, subject to the constant influence from organizational policies, goals, and structure, as well as peers and local fixers. The dynamics of negotiating newswork with these factors are structured by the power relations within the field of foreign correspondence as well as between the field and external fields of power, which are translated and structured into rules and norms.

Agents enter the field of foreign correspondence while accepting the basic rules of the game. These patterned, internalized rules are the semi-autonomous logic of the journalistic field (Benson, 2006). They are learned, shared, and passed down, as 'a powerful source of inertia' (Benson, 1999, p. 468), facilitating social control on journalists and their news practice, reproducing the existing power relations.

This chapter and the next chapter dive into the logic of the field of China correspondence, or in Bourdieu's language, the 'structure of the relations between the positions occupied by the agents or institutions who compete for the legitimate form of specific authority' (Bourdieu & Wacquant, 1992, p. 104). This chapter analyzes the journalistic logic at the organizational level, focussing on professional training as a newsroom control and the relational positions and autonomy of China correspondents in the news organizations. Chapter 5 examines the journalistic logic beyond organizational boundary, but of that in the field where the foreign press corps form a tribe, especially focussing on the routine practice of collective reference.

As the most common means of social control, organizational pressures exert critical influence on individual journalists and their news production in varying capacity. Different actors in the news organization, from journalists to editors to management, engage in negotiating a story and its presentation (Bailey & Lichty, 1972; Breed, 1955; Gans, 1979; Tuchman, 1978). The negotiation is shaped by the interplay of the news organizations' economic logic and journalistic logic, or the autonomy of the news organizations as against the broader field of power, embodied in the economic considerations of the news organization (Gans, 1979; Lesly, 1991; Sigal, 1973), ownership (Dunaway, 2008; Scott, Gobetz & Chanslor, 2008), news routines (Clayman & Reisner, 1998; Crouse, 1973; McCluskey, 2008; Sigal, 1973), as well as organizational structure (Breed, 1955; Gade, 2008).

'Position' is the key word here to understand the organizational control and journalists' routine practices in the newsroom. A news organization's position in the journalistic field and the capital it possesses decide the policy and goals of the news organization, as the positional pressure of news organizations is translated into newsroom values and norms (Bourdieu, 1998). Elite news organizations with massive cultural and symbolic capital embrace a more salient journalistic logic, whereas less privileged news organizations operate mostly on economic logic (or political logic in the case of the propagandist apparatus). 'Quality papers' such as *Le Monde, The New York Times*, and *The Guardian* occupy more cultural capital in a relatively autonomous position in the journalistic field. Within the newsroom, individual journalists in less autonomous positions feel stronger impetus to strictly follow the newsroom routines.

For news organizations, foreign reporting is a costly business. Especially with the changing media ecology in the digital age, the public consume news in a more diverse and dispersed way; consequently, the traditional news media platforms are losing appeal from advertisers, putting financial pressures on news organizations. The increasing conglomeration of international news media promise to further complicate the external pressures news organizations face. Of those with a prominent presence in international reporting, the *Financial Times*, for example, is now owned by Japan's Nikkei; Reuters has become part of Thomson Reuters, owned by the Canadian Thomson family with its headquarters in New York. The hybrid ownership of news outlets across journalism and non-journalism sectors, across different media formats, and across national borders is becoming intricate. It is high time to scrutinize how news organizations under increasing external pressures oscillate between journalistic and economic logic, and how such interplay is translated into organizational control on individual foreign correspondents.

This chapter mainly looks at the organizational control from the viewpoint of resource allocation, newsroom socialization, and editor-reporter relations, and how China correspondents negotiate their autonomy with these organizational pressures.

Organizational structure: resource allocation and socialization

Shoemaker and Reese (1996) rightly point out that organizational structure 'acts as a barrier or filter between the larger organization's economic requirements and the routines of newswork' (p. 139). It is to ensure the conformity of its members to its norms and policy. To understand the organizational mechanisms in bridging the organizational logic and the professional routines of individual journalists, one needs to first scrutinize the newsroom socialization and resource allocation within the news organization.

Organizational ideology and professionalism: social control in the newsroom

In Chapter 3, I discussed 'journalistic ideology' as part of journalistic habitus, bred in various media cultures and passed down through professional training, which includes both professional education and on-the-job learning. This on-the-job learning as an important source of journalistic ideology is realized through what van Ginneken (1998) identifies as the organizational-level socialization of journalists. They are expected to be familiar with and conform to the newsroom norms, rules, and goals.[1] This written or unwritten organizational ideology is what Chan and Lee (1988) note as 'one of the most important aspects of a news media organization's control' and helps to construct the journalistic paradigm (p. 194).

On newsroom social control, Soloski (1989) points out that, compared with explicitly elaborated rules and policies, professionalism is an efficient and economical method for social control in news organizations, by making 'the use of discretion predictable' (Larson, 1977, p. 168, cited by Soloski, 1989). As Breed (1955), Stark (1962), and Soloski (1989) found in their earlier classic studies on social control in the newsroom, all news organizations have rules and policies, but back then few news organizations had training programmes for newcomers, and social control was largely achieved through informal day-to-day contacts. After decades-long development of journalistic professionalism, a number of news organizations today reportedly provide various forms of training to better familiarize their new recruits with the organizational goals and norms, as well as to enable their assimilation of news professionalism. Tuchman (1978) asserts that 'professionalism serves organizational interests' (p. 12) and that journalistic professionalism is, in essence, 'knowing how to get a story that meets organizational needs and standards' (p. 66). AP's stylebook and Reuters' *Reuters Handbook of Journalism* are exemplars of such organizational control via professionalism training.

Both AP and Reuters are examples of *international media* or *transnational media*. At the time of writing, Reuters has 108 bureaus in 46 countries and AP has offices in 79 countries outside the United States. To make social control possible in these globally widespread newsrooms across various media cultures, these organizations have to ensure that their correspondents observe professional norms and values, with less reference to national context. Explicitly codified and culturally neutral professionalism training helps ensure organizational control in a transnational context.

Apart from the handbook, Reuters has a routine programme, 'Reuters Journalist Training,' to train new recruits directly out of university. It is a year-long intensive training on Reuters' editorial procedure and practice, by rotating new recruits onto different desks in its bureaus located worldwide. Its Beijing correspondent Paul Carsten, upon joining Reuters from the UK where he completed college, was first a trainee in bureaus in Bangkok and Singapore. Afterwards, he was appointed as a technology correspondent at the Beijing bureau.

For national media organizations, familiarity with home editorial values and policies is more important than codified professionalism training. Overseas correspondents of national news organizations usually have sufficiently assimilated professional values after years of working at national or metro desks at home. It could be assured that they, though working solo overseas, would still abide by the editorial policy of the news organization.

German national public radio network ARD puts their overseas correspondents on a month-long orientation trip, called '*ARD-Senderrundreise*' in German. All journalists assigned on overseas postings are required to hop on the orientation trip twice throughout their five-year contract: at the beginning of the posting and after two-and-half years into the posting. Correspondents would bounce between different stations from city to city throughout Germany, meeting editors and programme producers at ARD's more than 60 local stations. This is expected to help the correspondents to set up and maintain both professional and personal connections with editors, who are the effective 'gate keepers' of correspondents' filed stories, or 'to figure out what the different radio stations are expecting from their China correspondents,' as ARD Beijing correspondent Axel Dorloff explains. The aforementioned policy of many European news organizations to limit the length of overseas postings (see in Chapter 3) is also a means of maintaining foreign correspondents' adherence to organizational policy.

Professionalism training for organizational control is more prominent when a journalist switches between different news organizations. When Jaime FlorCruz joined CNN's Beijing bureau from *Time* magazine, he was put on a six-month voice training. While picking up new skills for a different media type, he also came to learn about the organizational policy and norms of CNN. FlorCruz recounts the difficulty for him while transitioning into a new organizational ideology:

> I remember in the first few months working for CNN, we would interview people, experts, [and] farmers in field. I would be sitting down with them, with a camera, [and] the producer. I would spend 30 minutes or 45 minutes with them, just as I would do for *Time*. Later my crew members told me you don't need to spend that much time with them. They [CNN] are used to talking to them [interviewees] for 10 minutes to get the sound bite they are looking for, and then move on. I didn't understand it at the beginning. So it is a different style of doing things.[2]

Apart from setting professional standards and norms, news organizations also substantialize newsroom social control through determining the professional reward system (Soloski, 1989). The recruitment and promotion pattern, or what Kornhauser (1963, cited by Soloski, 1989) calls 'the professional and management ladder,' socializes journalists to organizational goals and norms. Those high-valued journalists are rewarded either by an increase in salary and editorial autonomy (professional ladder) or by moving into the management hierarchy with greater authority (management ladder). More often, it is on the professional ladder rather than the management ladder that the journalists get their performance measured and rewarded institutionally. Shoemaker and Reese (1996) observe that in television stations, the promotion path to station management traditionally came through sales rather than editorial positions. This would condition the management to think in line with the economic logic. On the contrary, in some elite newspapers, editorial staff could be promoted to the top management. For example, *New York Times*' managing editor Joe Kahn had been the paper's China correspondent and international deputy editor. Such an appointment is widely understood as the paper's commitment to expanding its international coverage capacity (Ember, 2016). It sends a strong signal to its overseas correspondents regarding the organizational priority, which may facilitate the newsroom socialization of physically distant foreign correspondents.

Organizational resources allocation: beats structure

The structure of news organizations represents and shapes how journalists are assigned with and contend for scarce resources within the organizations. By allocating resources via certain organizational structures, media owners ensure social control in the newsroom (most famously argued by Breed in 1955). Of the organizational structure in newsrooms, the most basic arrangement of labour is the dispersion or allocation of reporters and editors in topics and space; in newsroom terminology, this labour division is called *beats* (Becker et al., 2000; Fishman, 1980; Tuchman, 1978). This organizational allocation of resources is the foremost definer of power relations at the organizational level in news production, 'the interplay of news professionalism and the resources of the news organization' (Soloski, 1989, p. 215). As in Tuchman's famous analogy of 'news net,' only with resources allocated can the occurrences be woven within the reach of the news net, thus have the chance to be selected to become news events.

Beats are 'geographic or topical in nature' (Becker et al., 2000). Journalists are dispersed to cover various places or topics (politics, trade, company, sports, etc.). But in foreign reporting, the nature of beats is usually a mix of space and topic. Covering China, for example, is both topical and geographic. China correspondents are foremost assigned to the 'China beat' at the geographic level of beats differentiation by their news organizations, in parallel to other overseas assignment in India, Japan, Kenya, etc. More resourceful news organizations further structure beats in their China reporting team either along the geographic line (Beijing, Shanghai) or topical line (Chinese politics, business news, social news, etc.). But as mentioned in Chapter 2, the geographic line within China is very much determined by the topical line.

Different beats are not necessarily equal in terms of the symbolic capital they each entail in the journalistic field. As Becker and his colleagues (2000) argue, beats can be ranked hierarchically and used as part of the managerial reward structure. In the case of China correspondents, especially for Sporadics or Spiralists (ref. Chapter 3), China is an important beat, but not as craved for as, for example, the US beat. Indian correspondent Ananth Krishnan said most Indian journalists would choose to be posted in the US, if they could. German correspondent Axel Dorloff also echoes the idea that the ideal posting would be in the US.

Beats enable news organizations to operate their organizational goals more efficiently (Becker et al., 2000) and help news organizations define individual journalists' autonomy and the spatio-temporal news net (Kim, 2003). A more centralized or hierarchical beats structure promises less autonomy for individual journalists.

Take the China reporting team of *The Wall Street Journal*: under Beijing Bureau Chief Charles Hutzler (at the time of this writing), there are at least two teams working on the politics beat and business beat, each headed respectively by a team leader (at the time of the writing, Jeremy Page leads the politics beat, under the title 'China political and diplomatic editor'; John Corrigan leads the business beat, under the title 'China business editor'). The team leaders are based in Beijing, while journalists in each team can be found in both Beijing and Shanghai. They establish and maintain news sources in the scope of their beat and decide on topics with their team leaders. In the case of a front page story, the story idea is pitched to the bureau chief, who then submits it to the New York-based editor for the final decision.[3]

News wires, operating on a strong economic logic, usually have a more hierarchical structure. In the Reuters Beijing office, management and editorial staff wear perplexing titles, including 'managing editor of Asia,' 'North Asia general manager,' 'Greater China bureau chief.' They share a huge open working space with dozens of senior and junior correspondents. Similar to *The Wall Street Journal*, the Reuters Beijing bureau assigns correspondents to different beats ranging from general news, company news, economics, and markets to commodity, in the form of teams. Each team has a senior correspondent as the leader, coordinating story selection and frames. Editorial meetings may not directly involve each reporter but are held throughout the day. Quite often Asian editors in Hong Kong also engage in daily discussion. Occasionally, the editor-in-chief in New York is consulted to make the final decision. 'The idea is to get things coordinated inside the bureau and globally,' said one senior editor at Reuters' Beijing office.

Although beats in these big news organizations 'become departments' (Becker et. al, 2000, p. 12), the boundaries between these departments are permeable. What Morrison and Tumber (1985) observed decades ago among London correspondents, that foreign correspondents are 'specialists in terms of journalistic labelling but generalists in practice,' still stands today among China correspondents. As the Reuters senior editor notes, 'most reporters do a bit of everything.'

Reuters technology correspondent Paul Carsten's assigned beat is technology report of Chinese IT companies. But from time to time he also covers various topics ranging from censorship and cyber security to geopolitics. Reporters in the newsroom can volunteer to ask for a certain assignment beyond their assigned beat, 'as long as you don't step on anyone's toes.'[4] Individual journalists can change their beat-defined titles while switching between news organizations with different beats structure. Sui-Lee Wee, a former political and general news correspondent with the Reuters Beijing bureau, turned to cover business in China for *The New York Times*.

Hierarchical beats structure tends to frustrate journalists who strive for more autonomy. Hence, among the foreign press corps in China, we observe a constant talent flow from heavily segmented and hierarchically structured news wires to more flat-structured newspapers or online news platforms. Correspondents having the job shifts are attracted by 'the luxury to decide on not just *what* to write, but also *how* to write,' and especially the luxurious time allowed for working on long investigative stories.[5] Michael Forsythe, having worked as the China correspondent for Bloomberg and later *The*

New York Times, credits the *Times* for 'absolutely more freedom to do pretty much any story you want to do.' Transitioning from seven-years reporting at Reuters to *The New York Times*, veteran China correspondent Chris Buckley also admits that he now enjoys more autonomy compared with the time at the Reuters.

One-person bureau: Sojos

Organizational control, via either professional training or beats structure, varies with newsroom size (Becker et. al, 2000). As maintaining a bureau is very costly for news organizations,[6] overseas newsrooms can be as small as a one-person bureau. Among China correspondents, more than one-third ($N = 206$) work alone in one-person bureaus.[7] Print media are mostly likely to operate a one-person bureau in China. Except for a handful of elite Anglo-American papers/newsmagazines and major Japanese papers,[8] all other print media deploy only one or two China correspondents.

This pattern is apparently not unique in China. Van Ginneken (1998) in examining the global news industry in general also notes that for larger American media, they usually have several correspondents with a small staff of assistants, whereas most European media usually only base a single staff correspondent on a posting, in a one-person bureau. In China, some other smaller European media organizations even choose to share one with another non-competing media. French journalist Eric Meyer covers China for three small European newspapers;[9] German journalist Johnny Erling reports for two German papers and one Austrian paper.[10]

Fleeson (2003) names journalists working alone in one-person bureaus as *Sojos*: solo journalists. Sojos have been common among correspondents with print media. In the broadcasting industry, thanks to the development of new ICTs, Sojos have become possible, replacing the old three-person crews (Gans, 2003). A solo broadcast journalist now can use a portable set of lightweight video camera and microphone to shoot most stories. With handy editing programmes and transmission tools, he/she can easily edit various versions of a news report, based on the specific length requirement from the programme editors, and file them to the headquarters in seconds. Yet resourceful Anglo-American and Japanese broadcasting media such as BBC, ABC (America), ABC (Australia), NBC, CNBC, CBS, CNN, NHK, and TBS still post traditional three-person or even larger crews in China.

Sojos generally perceive higher autonomy in their daily newswork.[11] To Indian correspondent Ananth Krishnan, who is a typical Sojo, autonomy is one of the biggest attractions for the profession of a foreign correspondent: '[I am] just completely independent . . . I can do whatever I want.'

But being bureaucratically freer in one-person bureaus is traded for more pinched resources, which may eventually undermine journalists' editorial autonomy. Due to heavy resource constraints,[12] Sojos do not only need to be generalists working on multiple beats, but they have to stretch themselves beyond China and cover the whole of Asia from time to time. NPR Beijing correspondent Anthony Kuhn frequently travels around greater China and even Southeast Asia. 'It's just too much to do. I'm spread very thin to a big number of countries,' Kuhn laments in a café in Beijing in late January of 2016. It was when he just finished a reporting trip in Hong Kong, regretting not being able to cover the Taiwan presidential election at the same time.

In addition to journalistic work, Sojos are burdened with many non-journalistic responsibilities, such as looking for an office space, hiring local helpers, and processing paperwork. Thus with the trade-off between resource constraints and a seemingly independent work mode, Sojos may not actually enjoy significantly higher autonomy as they do anecdotally.

In reality, Sojos are not that solo. They work with the assistance from local staff, 'fixers' or 'news assistants,' either on a full-time or part-time basis. By providing and facilitating local knowledge, translation, contacts, and access to people and places that are otherwise inaccessible, these local staff influence the vision and scope of the foreign correspondents (Murrell, 2014).

As I said earlier, in the field of China correspondence, Chinese nationals working for foreign media are not allowed to be accredited as 'journalists.' Instead, they wear the hat of 'news assistants,'[13] undertaking a wide range of duties from non-journalistic auxiliary work to real journalistic work including looking for story ideas, researching, and interviewing. An assistant-hiring ad by Canadian newspaper *The Globe and Mail* reads,

> The successful applicant will have a keen eye for the people and places that define this country to overseas audience, the tenacity to pursue difficult interviews, a talent for sifting out important information and a willingness to do a small amount of basic office management work.[14]

Foreign correspondents heavily rely on their local assistants not only for help in overcoming language and culture barriers, but also for local perspectives, as they help to 'illuminate the conditions in the country, the public mood, and political attitudes' (Oskenberg, 1994, p. 217). For Chris Buckley of *The New York Times*, news assistants contribute ideas and perspectives that might be easily overlooked by non-Chinese correspondents.

News assistants also facilitate access for foreign correspondents in the restrictive reporting environment of China. An Agence France Presse Beijing correspondent says, it is easier for Chinese news assistants to get access to interviewees and information. 'Many Chinese would agree to talk to a young Chinese, rather than some old foreign man,' says the Caucasian male journalist half-jokingly.

Some Chinese news assistants have been working in the same newsroom for decades, hence having accumulated invaluable connections and resources. The foreign correspondents themselves, on the contrary, come and go. This makes the correspondents even more heavily reliant on the veteran news assistants. This role of local news assistants is especially vital for Sojos. The ARD Shanghai bureau is led by Steffen Wurzel, a typical Sojo. He works with his news assistant who is a local Shanghainese working with the ARD Shanghai bureau for more than 10 years. The assistant's experience and rich connections contribute to ARD's China reporting in a noticeable way. During China's stock market plunge in January 2016, Wurzel was assigned by his editor in Germany to file a feature story about 'someone in the stock market.' Only in his second year in China, he had to entrust his news assistant to locate 'someone' for the interview. Although the stock market plunge was generally perceived as a signal for the overall slowdown of China's economic growth, his news assistant located a young Chinese woman who actually profited, rather than lost, from the stock market. The choice of interviewee, to a large extent, framed China's economy slowdown somehow positively.

Because of budgetary concerns, some less affluent non-Western one-person bureaus do not employ a full-time news assistant, yet the Sojos in these bureaus still work extensively with local assistants hired in a part-time mode. An Indian correspondent, while working on a story about a Chinese writer's controversial translation of the famed Indian poet Rabindranath Tagore's *Stray Birds*, had a part-time translator go through the Chinese writer's translation and tell him whether the translation was as 'vulgar' as many critics accused. Here, the translator became the key gatekeeper for the correspondent in framing the essence of the story.

In nationalism-fuelled ethnocentric China, Chinese nationals assisting foreign media can be bashed by the Chinese public for being unpatriotic or even a traitor, thus fit into the foreign-media-hostile narrative promoted by the Chinese government. Coercion on foreign press hence is often seen diverted to Chinese assistants, who have a higher stake in China's authoritarian system. Therefore, Chinese assistants can at times become a major concern for foreign correspondents to self-censor, if they do not want to risk their Chinese colleagues' safety. Chapter 6 will further discuss the state coercive apparatus targeting Chinese news assistants.

Autonomy in action: fighting against and dancing with editors

Journalists negotiate their autonomy with social control in the newsroom. Autonomy provides journalists 'room to claim professionalism and to both modify and ignore organizational rules' (Tuchman, 1978, p. 212). The most immediate actor they negotiate with every day is the editor, who functions as the intermediate between management and journalists (Soloski, 1989). Pedelty (1995) describes them as 'the most obvious and immediate symbol of institutional discipline' to 'facilitate the assimilation of institutional ideology into the individual journalist's regimen' (p. 90).

The role conflict between journalists and editors is inevitable, as journalists are more source-oriented whereas editors are concerned about audience interest and organizational goals (Gans, 1979; Shoemaker & Reese, 1996; Tunstall, 1971). These two divisions of labour in a news organization operate on different logics, with a different priority, thus almost ensuring daily power struggles.

The dynamics between editors and journalists are symbiotic. Apart from editing tasks, editors also manage people and resources (Underwood, 1988) and monitor, sometimes closely, the newswork of journalists. Journalists fight back to push the boundaries of their autonomous space and dance with the editors, especially on big investigative stories which require intensive organizational resources. The fight-dance negotiation is not an either-or scenario. As *New York Times* journalist Chris Buckley summarizes the editor-reporter covenant, 'They (editors) are my bosses; I have to take their viewpoints seriously; that's the starting point . . . but it's a more complicated process than either ignoring the editors or doing exactly what they say. It's a dialogue.'

Tell me what to do, not how to do it

In his seminal study on the newsroom of the US national networks and newsmagazines, Gans (1979) notes that journalists may only 'play a consulting role in story selection' but have more autonomy in story production (p. 101). My observation of the foreign press in China confirms the pattern: editors are effective in telling journalists *what* to do (story selection) but not in controlling them in *how* to do a story (story production).

Big news organizations such as international news wires usually draft a detailed agenda for a week, a month, or even a whole year. The senior editor of the Reuters Beijing office said they would set the 'priorities' of the whole year at the beginning of a new year. Speaking of their 2016 agenda when we met in November 2015 in Beijing, he names China's environment and economic reforms. In these big hierarchically structured news organizations, with relatively rigid plan implementation, journalists get assignments from the editors on a regular basis. The assignment requests are usually sent in a formal business email, rather than a personal email, avoiding personal dialogues and negotiation between individuals. 'You just have to do it. It's not a request. It's an order,' said one Agence France Presse correspondent.

When asked about the percentage of self-initiated stories versus editor-assigned stories, CNN's Jaime FlorCruz estimates about 80% or even more stories are pitched from the Beijing office rather than from editors in Atlanta (where CNN is headquartered), but live stories, mostly driven by breaking news, are largely decided by editors in Atlanta or Hong Kong, 'even if sometimes we think it's not that important.' German correspondent Axel Dorloff of ARD said half of his stories are initiated from the editors in Germany.

On rare occasions, the editors may go further to ask specifically for certain story elements, such as a street interview or even certain quotes. This is usually for big 'page one' stories, supplemented with contributions from correspondents in several overseas bureaus. When China was to modify its decades-old notorious one-child policy in late October 2015, *Hindustan Times* Beijing correspondent Patranobis was asked directly by his top editor to write a feature on the new policy. 'Usually he doesn't directly tell me what to do,' Patranobis recalls, but in this case the request came with a very detailed outline.

Although China correspondents' autonomy in topic selection is rather limited, they do enjoy considerable freedom during story production. Once the journalist and editor have reached the agreement on *what* to write, the final story is rarely 'killed' by the editor for disapproving *how* it is written.

Among the 101 survey respondents, a majority of them ($N = 71$, 70.3%) said their stories are 100% published/broadcast. Another 21.8% of the respondents ($N = 22$) said around 90% of their stories are finally published/broadcast. China correspondents' stories are rarely turned down by the editors, indicating they are generally entrusted with considerable editorial autonomy for news production. With such autonomy, some correspondents can even overturn the editors' pre-staged perspective.

Negotiating how with 'ignorant' general editors

Although most foreign correspondents only talk with one 'foreign news editor' at their home office, those in big news organizations usually have to deal with a hierarchical level of multiple editors. A simplified hierarchy of editors consists of two lines: those at home offices who probably have never been to China, and those based in Beijing, Shanghai, or Hong Kong, knowing China as well as, if not better than, the journalists. For easier discussion, I call the former *general editors*, and the latter *China editors*. These two types of editors, sitting on different hierarchies, engage in a different covenant with China correspondents.

Here let me first discuss the faraway general editors.

In the wake of the Paris Climate Talk in late 2015, an Agence France Presse China correspondent was asked by his editor in Paris to file a story on the carbon consumption of a typical Chinese 'second generation rich.' The editor explained to the correspondent that this would be part of AFP's series on global carbon consumption. This assignment was supposed to have a 'negative' touch, but the correspondent, having exchanged emails with this editor, managed to interview a Chinese *nouveau riche* who embraces the idea of low carbon living. This *nouveau riche* drives a luxury car but aims to exchange it for an energy-saving electric car; he runs three factories near Shanghai but claims they all meet the goal of 'zero emission.' The editor was not impressed by this 'not-as-negative-as-expected' perspective, and the correspondent explained that it was difficult to find someone who would fit the editor's sketch. In the end, the story was green lighted.

In this case, the China correspondent has the leverage to negotiate the perspective of the story with the general editor because he is in the field, whereas the editor is far away. Thus, the correspondent can cite the general editor's unfamiliarity with China and make use of his (presumed) Chinese habitus and capital to gain editorial autonomy. With this negotiated autonomy, he can take over the power to frame differently a specific story.

During my field interview with China correspondents in Beijing and Shanghai, the loudest complaints point to the general editors' ignorance about China: '[they are] sitting at the desk in New York, Paris, London, etc. . . . not knowing anything about China, yet telling us what to do!' Even in news organizations from East Asian countries, presumably with cultural proximity to China, correspondents are not impressed by their general editors' knowledge of China. This echoes Shoemaker and Reese's (1996) conclusion that 'reporters can counterbalance the power of the editor to the extent they have the support of their peers and greater firsthand knowledge of the subject matter than the editor' (p. 162).

NPR's Anthony Kuhn complains that his programme editors frequently ask for English-speaking interviewees in order to achieve better broadcasting effect, while Kuhn always tries to have interesting, authentic voices that are not necessarily the best English. 'If you always look for good English, you end up getting the same people all the time,' Kuhn lament.

Colombian journalist Villa Santiago spoke of China's grand military parade in September 2015 as an example of how the disagreement between him and his general editors on the significance of the event may undermine his newswork:

> I called them before the parade about its importance and they were not interested. Only a day after the parade they called me asking me to write a piece immediately. I could have done a good job with preparation, but not like that. . . . They would be interested in that only when

it became a big topic, all covered in the developed countries, then they will call me saying oh we want a story about it. But they won't take my suggestion to do the story before it proves to be a really big one.

Dancing in the same boat with China editors

In the case of Santiago, he is the lone warrior from his newspaper in the field, and even the only China-based journalist of the entire Colombian press. It is thus very difficult to convince editors to allocate organizational resources for him to work on big stories. But for larger news organizations with China editors and a squad of China correspondents in the field, they can garner personnel and budget to invest in a time-consuming investigative series which is usually led by an experienced China editor. As these heavily invested investigative stories easily stand out to be recognized or even award-winning, journalists who can gain huge symbolic capital are willing to dance in harmony with the editor.

On China's large-scaled and systematic crackdown on the Uyghur Muslim minority in Xinjiang, AP has been leading the global news coverage by an award-winning investigative series filed by its Beijing correspondent Gerry Shih.[15] But it was Shih's editor, AP's Beijing-based Greater China News Director Gillian Wong, who initiated and led the project, which was informed by Wong's own journalistic experience in China and interest in the topic before becoming an editor.[16]

In most cases, China correspondents and their immediate China editors share weal and woe. When a group of Bloomberg China correspondents were working on an investigative project titled 'Revolution to Riches'[17] on Chinese leaders' alleged financial scandals, Bloomberg management intervened under pressure from China. In 2013, a story was spiked by top editors during editing, and the lead journalist Michael Forsythe was suspended, setting off the resignation of a number of senior editors, including Forsythe's editor on the project Ben Richardson and Bloomberg's investigative department head Amanda Bennett.[18] This is when editors as the buffer zone between the business logic of the management and the journalistic logic lose, and so does the whole news organization. As Ben Richardson openly said, 'a small group of incompetent and self-serving managers have screwed things up for everyone else.'[19]

Star journalists

The reporter-editor covenant varies between different news organizations, and also varies between different agents occupying different positions in the field. Journalists with adequate capital take up a more autonomous position and are thus able to counterbalance editors or other sources of pressure. These powerful agents in the journalistic field are 'star journalists' (Breed, 1955; Sigelman, 1973). They are privileged with more capital, and thus have special autonomy to deviate to a certain extent from newsroom norms. They are the powerful agents with the capacity to challenge the norms or the power structures.

Wall Street Journal's senior correspondent and columnist Andrew Browne, for example, does not see his editorial autonomy constrained by any organizational pressures, especially not from editors. A veteran China correspondent with more than 30 years' reporting experience in Asia, he is also a Pulitzer Prize and Overseas Press Club award winner. These achievements bestow him enough symbolic capital to become a 'star journalist' in his organization and a 'powerful agent' in the field. 'No one tells me what to write,' Browne said. Unlike other *Wall Street Journal* China correspondents who are branded by specific beats such as 'China tech correspondent' or 'covering real estate in China,' Browne's Twitter profile states, 'I write about how China is changing your world.'

A veteran China correspondent of a European news agency says that if there is disagreement between him and his editors on how to report a story, he would just go the way he wants. 'I decide how to write it. . . . If you've been with a company for a while, there's a certain trust. They trust you in presenting the story in a proper way.' These powerful agents are not as constrained by organizational norms and pressures to conform, but to what degree they deviate to challenge the existing power structure is worth exploring yet not a focus of this book.

Conclusion

This chapter looks at the organizational control on China correspondents, including resource allocation, newsroom socialization, and editor-reporter relations, and how China correspondents negotiate their autonomy with these organizational pressures. News organizations use professional training, resource allocation, organizational structure, and most directly the reporter-editor covenant to ensure faraway foreign correspondents' daily work is constructive to the organizational goals. The correspondents as agents in the field actively negotiate their autonomy with organizational power players, in tactful pursuit for the opportunity to work on more career-rewarding stories. But as Breed (1955) has pointed out, their 'mobility aspiration' meanwhile drives them to conform to organizational constraints.

The myth of foreign correspondents as loners or Sojos does not guarantee more autonomy than working in bigger newsrooms with hierarchical labour division, as their autonomy is undermined by pinched resource constraints.

Instead, foreign correspondents' autonomy is more shaped by their position in the news organization and in the field (such as in the case of a star journalist of an elite news outlet).

It has to be acknowledged that, overall, foreign correspondents in China do enjoy relatively high autonomy. For example, in the editor-reporter relationship, although editors usually have more control in story selection, China correspondents have considerable autonomy in story production, benefiting from their local knowledge. Yet the problem of 'the eroding wall between newsrooms and boardrooms' (Hanitzsch et al., 2010) is grave in foreign newsroom operating in China. Although editors are doing what a former Reuters Beijing correspondent calls 'a Herculean job,' ideally shielding journalists from management pressure, the buffer zone between the business logic and journalistic logic does not always function well.

Besides the organizational pressures discussed in this chapter, ownership, for example, also influences correspondents' practice in a noticeable way. NPR's Anthony Kuhn notes that, compared with other journalists, he has more freedom to work on 'unorthodox' topics, such as folk music in China, because NPR is a public broadcaster, 'not government, not commercial . . . not as corporatized as other media.'

Organizational control is necessary not only for achieving organizational goals, but also for individual journalists to get professional guidelines or specific rules for playing the game. But its scale and power vary. In some cases, foreign correspondents from organizations with weak control psychologically suffer from 'too much freedom,' as they find themselves lacking direction (Hannerz, 2004; Morrison & Tumber, 1985). In continental European newsrooms, for example, organizational control via labour division and editor-reporter covenant is traditionally much weaker than in Anglo-American newsrooms (Donsbach & Paterson, 1992; Esser, 1998). A German correspondent in Shanghai complained about not having enough feedback from his editors: 'I was sometimes even frustrated.'

News organizations have their own organizational goals and logic, varying based on the quantity of all sorts of capital they possess and the heteronomous pressures from outside the organizations. In general, especially for the increasing complexity of media conglomerates, news organizations are sliding further towards a heteronomous pole. In the setting of China correspondence, foreign news organizations face more constraining external power to try to 'tame' the news content to the preference of the Chinese government. Chapter 6 discusses these external powers, mainly exerted by the Chinese government, and how China correspondents negotiate their autonomy with these external pressures.

Notes

1 As Soloski (1989) distinguishes between norms and rules, norms are unwritten, whereas rules are written news policies.
2 Personal communication, February, 2016.
3 Based on interview with the *Journal*'s senior correspondent Andrew Browne.
4 Personal communication with Paul Carsten in February, 2016.
5 Personal communication with Gerry Shih in January, 2018.
6 In the 2000s, it cost hundreds of thousands of dollars a year in correspondents' salaries, rent, and supplies, money for local staff, and $4,000 or $5,000 a month in travel expenses (Rieder, 2007).
7 Based on Foreign Press Directory (2015) issued by the Ministry of Foreign Affairs of China.
8 *The New York Times, The Wall Street Journal, The Washington Post, Financial Times, The Economist, The Daily Telegraph, El Pais, Mainichi Shimbun, Asahi Shimbun, Yomiuri Shimbun.*
9 *Les Dernières Nouvelles d'Alsace* and *L'Ouest-France* of France, and a Belgian paper *Le Soir.*
10 *Die Welt* and *Berliner Morgenpost* of Germany, and *Der Standard* of Austria.
11 A one-way ANOVA analysis of the survey data shows that Sojos perceive much weaker influence from management ($M = 2.09$, $SD = 1.13$) and newsroom peers ($M = 2.24$, $SD = 1.12$) than those working in larger sized newsrooms ($M = 2.67$, $SD = 1.12$ for management and $M = 2.89$, $SD = 1.08$ for newsroom peers), though there is no significant variance in perceiving influence from home editors between Sojos and non-Sojos.
12 Survey result shows Sojos perceive significantly stronger resource constraints ($M = 3.46$, $SD = 1.19$) than non-Sojos ($M = 3.02$, $SD = .95$).
13 Other titles include 'researchers,' 'analysts,' or 'producers,' varying in different news outlets.
14 From *Globe and Mail* Beijing correspondent Nathan VanderKlippe.
15 The series 'China's Uighurs: On Edge' can be found at https://www.apnews.com/China'sUighurs
16 See www.nytco.com/gillian-wong-joins-international/
17 Bloomberg has removed the series from its online archive. But being recognized by the Society of Publishers in Asia (SOPA) awards in 2013, the series can be found on the SOPA archive here: https://2013.sopawards.com/wp-content/uploads/2013/05/45-Bloomberg-News1-Revolution-to-Riches.pdf
18 Roush, C. (November 13, 2013). Pulitzer winner Bennett leaving Bloomberg. Retrieved from https://talkingbiznews.com/1/pulitzer-winner-bennett-leaving-bloomberg/
19 Wong, E. (March 25, 2014). Ex-Bloomberg editors tells why he left. Retrieved from https://sinosphere.blogs.nytimes.com/2014/03/25/ex-bloomberg-editor-tells-why-he-left/

5   Reporting as a tribe
Journalistic logic in collective interpretation

Foreign correspondents in the field need to seek frames of reference, social support, a sense of belonging in a tribe. Hence, the journalistic logic is not confined to organizational norms or journalistic professionalism, as discussed in Chapter 4. Beyond news organizations, within the tribe of foreign correspondents, in order to compare with peers for either verification or ideation, they tend to reach out to fellow correspondents on a frequent basis. Foreign correspondents in the field form what Zelizer (1993) calls an interpretive community, where journalists collectively make sense of news events. Between the tribe and external forces, especially censorship, the sense of community is not just figurative but is also an actual collective action to cooperate and support each other, so to maintain the journalistic autonomy of the profession in highly restrictive China.

Members of the press corps are both competitors and accomplices. They may compete for resources and capital, but they also cooperate to fight against external pressures (criticism) that pose imminent threats to their autonomy. An 'esprit de corps' does exist in the foreign press corps, especially when being pressured hard by Chinese authorities. This is when they feel the need to form a kind of collective to help maintaining the autonomy, if any, of the whole field of foreign correspondence.

This chapter continues the line of journalistic logic. It looks into the foreign press corps in China as an interpretative community formed on the basis of nationality and colocation (geographic proximity), and how this community is going ambient thanks to the prevalence of digital technology (social media) and inter-media mutual validation of a shared discourse. Chapter 6 will focus on how this community counters external censorship and coercion in China.

Press review as a professional necessity

The interpretative community of journalists relies on 'shared interpretations' (Zelizer, 1993, p. 224) created via routinized press review and other less routinized informal talks, memoirs, etc. Press review is the routinized journalistic practice of the community, the most prominent in the field of foreign correspondence, where journalists cluster around the same news site, rely on each other for sources and local knowledge, and are very likely to be chasing the same stories.

To understand press review as a doxic journalistic logic in the interpretative community of journalists, we should first distinguish press review from the much-denounced notion of 'pack journalism.' The latter is a commonly shared criticism on herds of journalists clustering around the same news site and 'engage[ing] in copycat reporting by using and sharing news information, and lazily refrain[ing] from confirming the data through independent sources' (Matusitz & Breen, 2012, p. 897).[1] Press review, on the other hand, as Bourdieu (2005) and Champagne (1999) define it, is the routine practice of journalists to constantly follow the coverage of peers, both colleagues and competitors, to situate themselves in a position that will distinguish them from their competitors. It is about positioning: the positioning of one story in relation to other stories; the positioning of one journalist in relation to other journalists; and the positioning of the news organization in relation to other news organizations (Schultz, 2007).

In a similar vein, Boczkowski (2010) calls it newspeople's 'imitation' and 'monitoring practice.' Admittedly, it risks resulting in homogeneity in news content as a flock of journalists pursue the same news sources to cover the same story, and such practice undermines the diversity of a healthy journalism. However, it is a 'professional necessity' (Champagne, 1999 [1993], p. 47), the inevitable result of a power struggle in the journalistic field, where agents compete for limited resources on deadline (see e.g. Schultz, 2007). Van Ginneken (1998) categorizes such press review practice as one thread of journalists' tertiary socialization on the job, after the primary socialization at culture level and the secondary socialization at profession level. Peer journalists, as van Ginneken (1998) argues, function as each other's prime reference group, hence the act of reviewing or monitoring each other's work.

Bourdieu (1998) in *On Television* argues that in journalistic production, journalists are largely subject to collective pressures, especially competitive pressures. Their daily routine, such as daily review of the press every morning, is 'one of the mechanisms that renders journalistic products so similar,' and 'this is an effect typical of the field: you do things for competitors that you think you're doing for consumers' (p. 24–25). Deviating from the consensual line risks criticism from government, advertisers, and peer news organizations, hence agents (journalists and news organizations) tend to avoid such deviation by closely watching others' practice, which usually, yet not always, results in inter-institutional conformity or so-called pack journalism. Thus, pack journalism can be seen as the undesired potential result of the professional necessity of press review.

Competition, positional pressures: differentiation and de-differentiation

As aforementioned, the dynamic of such collective reference is the need to position oneself (either individual journalist or news organization) in relation with competitors, so to distinguish oneself or differentiate from others. Foreign correspondents tasked with different national markets at home countries tend to subscribe to the dominant logic of the field and lose their autonomy, thus 'de-differentiating' themselves to consolidate their positions and preserve the field (Tandoc, 2017). The strategies of differentiation or de-differentiation depend on the positional pressures to which agents are subjected. Either way, foreign correspondents closely watch competitors, and sometimes non-competitors (for example, many continental European or non-Western correspondents closely follow major Anglo-American media organizations, even though they are not competitors), in order to make sure that they didn't miss any 'significant' story and to consolidate or elevate their positions in the field.

A Shanghai-based veteran European correspondent's comment is typical of such routine 'monitor for competition' practice:

> Everyone watches what everyone else's doing. There's definitely examples of competitive pressure to do it . . . there's definitely 'pack journalism,' or 'group journalism,' where you see someone doing something and you do it because they are doing it. So the judgment is not necessarily news value. It's 'they are doing it, so we do it.'[2]

In China reporting during the past decade, the most high-profile example of such collective reference on topics might be the wave of investigative stories during 2012 and 2013 on China's high-ranking Party leaders' corruption and hidden family wealth. Chinese top leaders' families are traditionally a taboo topic for both Chinese domestic media and foreign media. But the year of 2012 witnessed an unusual pack reporting vying to investigate and reveal the long-held taboo topic among leading Anglo-American media organizations including *The Wall Street Journal*, Bloomberg, and *The New York Times*.

The stormy unprecedented pack investigation started from early February of 2012, the year of leadership transition in China. In an astonishing move, the then police chief of Chongqing Municipal in southwest China fled to seek refuge in the US consulate, amid escalated clashes with Bo Xilai, then Party chief of Chongqing Municipal and Politburo member, widely believed to be a potential appointee for the highest leadership of the country. A week later, the Hong Kong-based magazine *Next* first broke the story of the secret family wealth connection of Bo's family (Coronel, 2012). The story of the most scandalous purge of Chinese top officials was soon followed up by major Western news organizations, including *The Wall Street Journal*, *The New York Times*, and Bloomberg. *The Wall Street Journal* took the lead among others in uncovering the family corruption of this political superstar of China, having published a well-received profile on Bo's wife on April 7, 2012.[3] The article, referring to Bo's wife as the 'Jackie Kennedy of China,' unveils her complex financial ties, both in China and abroad, and how she is allegedly responsible for the death of British businessman Neil Heywood.

Competing news organizations, represented by Bloomberg News and *The New York Times*, then had to divert their focus onto different individual top-level political figures, to distinguish themselves from the *Journal*'s scoop while not missing out in the thematic dirt-digging.

Then *New York Times*' Shanghai correspondent David Barboza later broke an investigative story on then outgoing Prime Minister Wen Jiabao's family business,[4] which landed him the Pulitzer Prize for international reporting of 2013 for the *Times*. Bloomberg's Michael Forsythe and his colleagues worked on a series of the power and fortune of China's 'Eight Immortals' or red nobility, including President Xi Jinping's family,[5] aiming for a Pulitzer Prize as well. A Bloomberg editor recalled how the investigation team decided to dig into Xi's family fortune: 'We came to the conclusion that we should stop trying to look where the *Journal* and the *Times* were looking, Xi is fair game. . . . That's why we started looking at Xi Jinping' (French, 2014).

In a salad house next to *the New York Times*' Hong Kong office, Michael Forsythe explained to me how, as then Bloomberg's China correspondent leading the investigative stories, he and his colleagues set their mind on the topic. When the *Wall Street Journal*'s story on Bo Xilai broke out, they felt huge competitive pressure. 'How do we distinguish ourselves from them?' Inspired or pressured by the *Journal*'s investigation on Bo, Forsythe and his colleagues followed up to investigate the wealth of Bo's wife and the family of his wife, and then all nine members of the highest Standing Committee of the Politburo. Soon they had some exciting findings on the enormous fortune of Xi's sister. 'Bo Xilai scandal refocused everybody's attention. Suddenly Chinese politics, high politics, became interesting again. . . . Suddenly, it became a priority [for news media].'

Wall Street Journal's senior China correspondent and columnist Andrew Browne echoes that competition leads to the pack investigation: 'That [the

Journal's report on Bo Xilai] was very closely followed by our rivals – the *New York Times*, the Bloomberg, so they came after Wen Jiabao and Xi Jinping.'[6]

This wave of investigative reports targeting China's highest political leaders finally ebbed due to the huge political and economic pressures the Chinese government swiftly exerted on these three news outlets and their China correspondents. Both the *Times* and the *Journal* had their business in China severely undermined. The *Times*' websites, including its newly launched Chinese-language website, were blocked as a 'punishment,' and its incoming China correspondents have been denied visas for three years. As mentioned in Chapter 4, Bloomberg conceded to such pressure by killing another upcoming story on Xi Jinping's family connection with the richest business tycoon of China,[7] but the company suffered in the way of compromising its journalistic integrity and reputation. Maybe critics can blame Bloomberg for not having behaved tougher in the negotiation with pressures from China, but it needs to be acknowledged that such investigative journalism requires considerably high autonomy of the news organizations in the field. Most news organizations, such as Bloomberg with a huge business stake in the China market, are evidently residing toward the heteronomous pole as to their position in the field of China correspondence.

This is a typical example of powerful agents acting under positional pressures to transform the dynamics in the field. Journalists in the field struggle and compete for more capital, especially symbolic capital (such as winning a Pulitzer). The case of the three American media organizations vying for scoops on the corruption of China's elite is a painstaking fight between journalistic autonomy and external power control from political and economic forces. Media outlets such as *The New York Times* enjoy much higher autonomy in the field, yet after struggling with the external power control, the dynamics and norms within the field are rebalanced back to its original configuration, deviated little from the previous power structures. As some critics observe, after that breathtaking wave of scoops, the public have not seen the emergence of many more reports of that genre. The foreign media coverage on China went back to staying away from the taboo topic of the top leadership.

The competitive pressure to join the pack sometimes can be repelling – correspondents despise certain stories but have to (or are told by editors to) cover simply because their competitors have carried the said stories. This is when correspondents have to 'de-differentiate' for fear of deviation, though they risk compromising their autonomy. *India Today* Beijing correspondent Ananth Krishnan complains about the situation when he *had to* cover a 'survey' launched by the Chinese jingoistic tabloid *Global Times* asking its readers to rank their favourite neighbouring countries.

Given the delicate relations among China, India, and Pakistan, it was a complicated and sensational topic for the Indian press, especially as the *Global Times*' readers overwhelmingly favour Pakistan over India.[8] Krishnan himself dismisses the so-called survey as 'dubious' and 'self-selecting,' thus was at first reluctant to report on it. But when PTI, India's biggest news wire, covered the survey, followed by many other Indian media, he knew he *had to* cover it. 'Unfortunately I couldn't ignore the story'; Krishnan was obviously not proud of having filed the story. He takes on the competitive pressures: 'If your competitors are doing it, you can't be an ostrich; you can't bury your head in the sand and say it's beneath me. My newspaper can't miss a story if other newspapers are going to have it.'

'Source review': collective pool of sources

Besides collective reference on what to report, collective reference on news sources is another prominent routine practice of China correspondents under positional pressures. Foreign correspondents' source pool in the host country is limited, and it is especially true in the increasingly censored society of China. For a source to meet the requirement of authority, credibility, and availability (van Ginneken, 1998) can be rare. Working on deadline, China correspondents tend to turn to the same sources repeatedly, instead of investing time and resources to find other sources; when they do not have known routine sources for a story, they reach out to those existing sources quoted in their peers' stories via what I call 'source review,' parallel to 'press review.' This practice of routine and collective source can be understood in what Revers (2017) notes as 'collective wisdom,' the exchange or sharing of background knowledge and connections, though not always active sharing.

Beijing-based China correspondents to a certain extent resemble the campaign press corps described by Crouse (1973), routinely going back to the same sources from embassies, Foreign Ministry, press conferences, and state media such as Xinhua and *People's Daily*. Foreign Ministry, acting as the main official source venue for foreign correspondents, has been holding a daily press conference on weekdays since 2011.[9] Even though the Ministry provides a 24-hour contact number for press inquiry, foreign correspondents seldom find these numbers accessible in practice. A European correspondent complains, 'even if you call the number, usually they don't answer your question until the [press] briefing is held.' Such restrictive official sources only intensify journalists' practice of source review.

Expert sources are also increasingly cramped under the tight ideology and speech control by the current leadership in China. Correspondents keep consulting the same small pool of experts on China policy, but few Chinese experts are included in this source pool. As van Ginneken (1998) observed decades ago, 'an "old China hand" is almost never a Chinese' (p. 100). Things remain unchanged today.

In covering the surprising removal of top-level Party official Sun Zheng-cai in July 2017, major Anglo newspapers mostly cited Western *China experts* instead of *Chinese experts* on analyzing Chinese elite politics.

Table 5.1 shows the number of expert sources used by China correspondents with major Anglo-American newspapers covering Sun's removal. Though it seems that correspondents are trying to maintain a balance between Chinese and Western expert sources (for example, *The New York Times* and the *Financial Times* quoted the same number of Chinese and Western experts), Western sources are yet still the majority. Of all the 10 expert sources, only two are China-based Chinese experts.

The three expert sources *The Guardian* cited are US expert Susan Shirk, Brookings Institute's China Center director Cheng Li, and Bill Bishop, a veteran China watcher and US-based publisher of the Sinocism newsletter on China affairs. All three sources are in effect American experts (Cheng Li is a Chinese American). Susan Shirk, a former high-ranking official, is also one of the two non-Chinese expert sources cited in the *New York Times* article on the same topic published one day earlier. Similarly, Bill Bishop is a routine source repeatedly cited by major Anglo media outlets including Reuters, *Financial Times*, and *The Washington Post*. He is seen, for example, talking about the North Korea crisis and US-China relations in *The Washington Post*,[10] China's artificial intelligence technology in the *Times*,[11] and China's policy change toward US consulting companies in *Financial Times*.[12] His biography on his Sinocism website is probably more intuitively telling: '[I] am often quoted in major media such as Bloomberg,

Table 5.1 Number of Expert Sources Cited in Mainstream Anglo-American Newspaper

Newspaper	Date	No. of expert sources	No. of Chinese expert sources (China-based)	No. of non-Chinese expert sources
The New York Times	July 24	4	2 (1)	2
The Wall Street Journal	July 17	0	0 (0)	0
The Guardian	July 25	3	1 (0)	2
Financial Times	July 25	2	1 (1)	1
The Daily Telegraph	July 25	1	0 (0)	1
Total		10	4 (2)	6

Financial Times, *Wall Street Journal*, Reuters, *New York Times*, *The Guardian*, etc.'[13] This is also an illustrative example of the symbiotic relationship between journalists and sources (Carlson, 2009; Gans, 1979). While legitimizing certain frames for the media, the routine source also is legitimized for his/her/its own status and capital accumulation.

Veteran China correspondents have established their own connections with sources, including official sources and expert sources. New entrants, lacking such resources and capital and under positional pressures, tend to look for veteran correspondents' sources if they are traceable and available. Former *HuffPost* China correspondent Matthew Sheehan admits that he did not have much local connection in China. What he did is to contact those routinely quoted in other correspondents' stories and thus develop them into his own sources, as 'they are usually happy to talk on record.' As for me, after having been quoted on record in a *New York Times* story on the #MeToo movement in China, I have been contacted by at least two journalists working for different foreign news organizations for comment on the same topic. In both cases, the journalists told me they traced me down from the *New York Times* story.

By collective reference in news sources, the elite status of those routine sources are reproduced and consolidated, and so is the symbiotic and symbolic journalist-source relationship. Or, in a nutshell, the power structure in the field is reproduced and enhanced. Routine sources have their cultural power reinforced and augmented through constant media access.

Colocation and collective reference

Boczkowski (2010) identifies colocation and content availability as the two salient factors in understanding the degree of imitation or monitoring practice in journalism. Crouse's (1973) account of 'notorious pack journalism' of election campaign reporters packing in the campaign bus is an extreme case of such colocation. Chapter 2 has sketched the geographic spread of China correspondents, who are not exactly Crouse's 'boys on the bus,' but do usually share the same geographic space, thus tend to huddle together to form the interpretative community in substance.

Hannerz (2004) in his study on foreign correspondents on a global scale records that they are segmented and loosely structured along nationality, physical proximity, and types of beats. As to physical proximity, foreign correspondents' offices are more likely to concentrate in local space.

China correspondents in Beijing follow a similar pattern. Before the 1990s, all foreign media operating in China were designated to live and work first in two hotels and then in diplomatic compounds in the diplomatic district in east Beijing (Chen & Wang, 2009; Qian, 2015). Today most

Western media still base their offices in the area where foreign embassies and Chinese ministries are concentrated. The Ministry of Foreign Affairs of China, foreign correspondents' supervising body in China, is also close by, making it logistically easier for correspondents to attend press conferences or visit the International Press Center.

The six diplomatic compounds[14] housing most foreign news organizations are located within around four kilometres of each other, adjacent to the most vibrant and cosmopolitan area in Beijing. Piles of popular restaurants, cafes, and bars in the area offer comfort and convenience for foreign correspondents to socialize among themselves as well as with sources and local connections. The Bookworm is a popular bookshop doubled up as a library and bar among locals and expatriates, where many cultures intersect. It has a huge collection of English-language books on China and Asia studies and regularly hosts literary and cultural events, making it an exceptional spot in Beijing. Many English-speaking foreign correspondents frequent this place not just for meeting sources and connections, but also because it is a collective knowledge-sharing venue, where they may attend seminars or panels discussing a wide range of topics about China together with fellow correspondents and China watchers of other professions.[15] The Foreign Correspondents Club of China (FCCC) organizes almost all events in this compact neighbourhood. All of my face-to-face interviews except one during a two-month field observation in Beijing were done in that area.

Reuters and Bloomberg, the two major financial news wires, are understandably located slightly outside the diplomatic district. Their Beijing bureaus, each with dozens of reporters and outnumbering most foreign news outlets, are set upon the 'Beijing Financial Street,' close to activities of main financial regulatory commissions and banks.

Most China correspondents work in small newsrooms which are geographically concentrated. Sojos of the same or similar national context tend to share work space. All public broadcasting media from Scandinavia (Danish TV, Swedish TV, and Norwegian NRK) share one office space in one of the diplomatic compounds. German news organizations are mostly based in the same compound or the same building, networking among themselves professionally and socially on a daily basis. For the daily press conference of the Foreign Ministry, they would share a taxi ride together. This is not just out of financial concern. More importantly, as Qian (2015) cites a Sojo European correspondent who shares an office in Beijing with several other Sojos of different European news organizations, working solo every day without casual communication with peers may undermine their journalistic sensitivity in a host country. Some freelancers rent a workstation in a shared office with other staff correspondents. Such colocation in work space makes sure freelancers stay close to the positions they are aiming to acquire.

Colocation risks homogenizing how journalists interpret events into news, because of convenience in resource sharing and cooperation. On December 2, 2015, when Beijing issued the first ever air pollution Red Alert, I was visiting some of the foreign media's offices at the Dongzhimen Diplomatic Compound. On the street outside the compound, within the short distance of about 500 metres, three batches of foreign TV media staff, from both Asian and Western countries, were shooting the smog story in the grey, choking air. Thus, on that day, audiences watching TV in different corners of the world were fed with similar shots on the same street about China's pollution. Revers (2017) specifies that both collective agenda setting and collective interpretation of issues are basic forms of pack journalism. In this case, as the immediate social setting is conveniently shared, pack journalism in both forms (collective agenda setting and collective interpretation) is almost guaranteed.

Interpretative community going ambient

Hargreaves (2003) and Hermida (2010) have respectively argued for the concept of 'ambient news' and 'ambient journalism,' referring to the ubiquitous nature of news consumption and production. Digital technologies, especially social media, have augmented the scale of foreign correspondents' interpretative community. Boczkowski (2010) notes an increase in technology-assisted means and a decrease in face-to-face encounters of journalists to follow stories their peers and competitors are working on. Echoing the pattern, China correspondents are also observed increasingly reliant on digital platforms to look for reference and legitimize themselves, in effect pushing the interpretative community going ambient.

Twitter, for example, is defined by Hermida (2010) as computer-mediated awareness systems to assist its users in constructing and maintaining meanings 'even when the participants are not co-located' (Markopoulos et al., 2009). From the geographically restricted tribe which is mainly found in Beijing to as extended as the internet could be, Beijing-based China correspondents can easily form a virtual community with their peers based in Shanghai, Hong Kong, or other cities in China, and with China watchers overseas.

Twitterized tribe of China correspondents

Of all social media platforms, Twitter might be the most important and most widely used by journalists for professional work (Hedman, 2015). Almost all China correspondents from English-language news organizations (the US, UK, Australia, Canada, and India) have an active presence on Twitter. Of the surveyed China correspondents, 59.4% actively use Twitter as one of the self-promotion platforms. This makes Twitter a convenient window for journalists to monitor their competitors. NPR Beijing correspondent

Anthony Kuhn notes one of the ways for him to know what his peers are working on is to follow their tweets.

Apart from publishing their own articles, China correspondents discuss China's policies, social problems, novelties – almost all topics – on Twitter, and quite possibly, they take on a story idea from their Twitter discussion. This is the extension of journalistic interpretative community discourses going to the front stage from the backstage (Mourão, 2015). Zeng and Song (2018), in their study on 127 China correspondents' use of Twitter, found that China correspondents on Twitter primarily network with other journalists from both China beats and beyond, from both their own home countries and other countries, notably expanding the previously identified pattern of foreign press corps structured along nationality, physical proximity, and types of beats.

But this Twitterized community may conveniently foster groupthink and, as Zeng and Song (2018) note, 'graft pack journalism onto new emerging practices.' Former *HuffPost* China correspondent Matthew Sheehan observes 'a dangerous groupthink mentality on Twitter' among China correspondents.[16] A typical example is Western media's flocking coverage on a racist Chinese video targeting India.

China's state news agency Xinhua, on August 16, 2017, released a video titled 'Seven Sins of India,' bashing India for the ongoing Doklam border standoff between the two countries. The video had a Chinese actor playing an Indian, dressed in traditional turban and mocking the Indian accent. The video was soon branded 'racist' and tweeted by *India Today* Beijing correspondent Ananth Krishnan, who has more than 25,000 followers on Twitter, among them many China correspondents or China/India watchers. This tweet was retweeted more than 200 times and sparked wide criticism of Xinhua almost with no delay. Apart from the Indian media, major Anglo media including *The New York Times*,[17] BBC,[18] *Financial Times*,[19] and *The Washington Post*[20] soon followed up, all quoting condemning Indian journalists' tweets as a source. Both *The New York Times* and BBC directly quoted from Krishnan's tweet.

Yet this Twitterized tribe is largely restricted to English-speaking journalists, especially Western journalists. Journalists from other countries and cultures are not avid users of Twitter for reasons of language, habits, and company rules. For example, most Japanese media do not allow their staff to run their own personal social media accounts, Twitter accounts included.

The web of inter-validation

China correspondents in the ambient interpretative community inter-validate each other's discourse of China stories, and inter-validate with experts or professionals from non-journalistic fields, by ways of engaging in other news organizations' discourse construction, sharing and negotiating perspectives with a wider range of social actors in public talks or online forums.

Between non-competitive news organizations, foreign correspondents share their knowledge on each other's platforms, strengthening the collective discourse construction at the inter-media level. China correspondents are seen or heard as guest speakers on China topics at other foreign news organizations. Agence France Presse Beijing correspondent Joanna Chiu has been interviewed by NPR, ABC, and BBC on topics ranging from China's strategy in the South China Sea and the US-China trade war to the pro-democracy movement in Hong Kong and the #MeToo movement in China.[21]

China correspondents extend their authority in the ambient interpretative community by way of other platforms such as blogs and podcasts that engage actors from various fields beyond the journalistic field. These platforms can be individual start-ups (such as the popular podcast *SupChina*) or institution-initiated projects (such as online magazine *ChinaFile*, published by Asia Society). Most of these platforms are founded and led by former journalist-entrepreneurs or journalist-academics who switch between different fields. They serve as a public arena for collective deliberation and interpretation on China topics, connecting generations of China correspondents, academics, and politicians, effectively facilitating and validating the media's collective discourse on China.

Take *ChinaFile*. Its publisher is award-winning journalist-academic Orville Schell, who reported on China for the *New Yorker* in the 1970s and has published 10 books on China; Susan Jakes, former China correspondent for *Time* magazine, serves as its editor. It has more than 300 regular contributors, including former and current China correspondents, academics, activists, writers, lawyers, and entrepreneurs, from both China and the rest of the world. The platform hosts weekly conversation, engaging discussants from the abovementioned fields. A discussion on Xi Jinping's 'personal cult' in 2016 presented scholars from universities, think tanks, activists, and journalists. These openly available discussions provide China correspondents with convenient reference and expert sources, consolidating the ambient interpretative community.

A Factiva search on news articles explicitly citing '*ChinaFile*' in the year of 2016 generated more than 30 articles from leading newspapers and wires in the U.S (e.g. *The New York Times*, *The Washington Post*), Australia (e.g. *The Australian Financial Review*), Britain (e.g. *Financial Times*), Canada, France, Spain, Japan, Singapore, Denmark, and Zimbabwe. These articles either reported on an extensive dataset compiled by *ChinaFile* on China's anti-corruption campaign or quoted from the research articles or interviews published on *ChinaFile*. *The Australian Financial Review*, for example, published a long piece titled 'The Cult of Xi Jinping' on March 24, 2016, quoting a scholar discussant in the *ChinaFile*'s weekly conversation on the exact topic weeks earlier.[22]

'*The New York Times* disease'?

As positional pressure is the key dynamic behind the collective reference practice of the interpretative community of China correspondents, there is no doubt a hierarchical structure in the community. Those news organizations or correspondents with more capital, especially cultural/symbolic capital, often take the lead setting the frame of reference. Other agents, feeling the positional pressure against those powerful agents, closely follow suit. Anglo-American media are the powerful ones with huge capital and thus take more autonomous positions. A German correspondent in Beijing admits that 'international leading news organizations are mostly American plus BBC.'[23]

Of all the Anglo-American media, *The New York Times*, self-professed 'newspaper of the record,' is widely acknowledged as on the top of the professional hierarchy (see e.g. Gitlin, 1980). Golan (2006) found that *The New York Times* set the agenda of international news for the three major networks of the US; Pedelty (1995) even uses '*The New York Times* disease' to refer to the self-referential and agenda-setting tendencies of *New York Times* correspondents in their coverage of the Salvadoran War. As Pedelty explains, *New York Times* correspondents 'play an institutional role in defining the national, and sometimes international, news agenda' (p. 73). Such agenda-setting capability of *The New York Times* is also noted by other scholars such as Rosenblum (1979). Thus, news narratives become what Pedelty calls '*Times*-sanctioned truth.'

Likewise, in the field of China correspondence, journalists overwhelmingly view *The New York Times* as leading the hierarchy. Figure 5.1 shows the leading news organizations rated by China correspondents.[24] Anglo-American media clearly take the absolute lead. But a national variance is observed. German and Austrian journalists, for example, tend to rate their own German-language elite media (*Der Spiegel, Die Welt, Die Zeit*) as the most influential players in the field of China reporting. This national variance is because journalists of the same national context share the same national market as well as cultural affinity. Thus, they tend to cluster together and monitor each other more closely. Korean journalists, for example, even have their own professional and social club in China.

The degree of such collective practice also varies across countries. A more 'pack-minded' press corps is observed from Liberal countries and

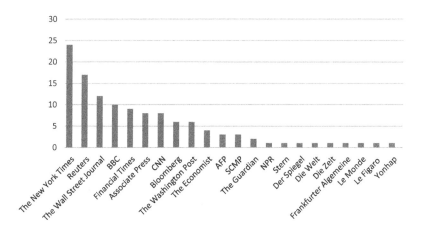

Figure 5.1 Hierarchy of News Organizations as Rated by China Correspondents

Democratic Corporatist countries, where the media market and journalistic professionalism are more mature.[25] Correspondents from these countries thus form a more cohesive 'interpretive community' in the field. The afore-mentioned story on China's Xinhua racist video against India, for example, is not covered by any of the three mainstream Japanese newspapers.[26] Nei-ther was the ousted Sun Zhengcai story.

At an individual level, most journalists are reluctant to name any indi-vidual correspondents whom they consider more influential than others. Among those names popping up, *New York Times* Beijing correspondent Chris Buckley notably stands out, though he was named primarily by his peers from Anglo-American news organizations, with whom he shares a similar audience and market. His leading role as the frame of reference in the field of China is acknowledged by *SupChina* as 'China journalists' China journalists.'[27]

As a typical Sinophile, Buckley's outstanding local knowledge and con-nections already land him in an advantageous position in the field. But tra-ditionally, journalists in print news are less salient than their colleagues in television news (Hannerz, 2004, p. 147), and Buckley is not even an award-winning journalist. Yet he represents *The New York Times*. The fact that Buckley is voted as the influential tone-setter suggests the positional competitiveness of organizations may be translated to positional power of its representatives. His institutional affiliation with *The New York Times* undoubtedly builds up another asset of symbolic capital, which helps to place him in a higher and more autonomous position.

Conclusion

This chapter focuses on the collective reference practice of China correspondents from Zelizer's (1993) perspective of interpretative community. The collective discourse on China stories are achieved through position-driven differentiation and de-differentiation. In an effort to consolidate or elevate their positions, China correspondents either differentiate or de-differentiate themselves from peer journalists as their important reference group.

The routine practice of press review as collective reference is a professional necessity, largely defined by colocation and nationality. Journalists of the same or similar national context tend to form a cohesive community either for professional or social function. The positional pressures are stronger among journalists competing for the same audience, thus collective reference is more salient among journalists of the same national context. Overall, elite Anglo-American news organizations such as *The New York Times* unsurprisingly take the lead in the community. What Pedelty (1995) calls '*The New York Times* disease' can find some trace in the community of China correspondents, though I would hesitate to use the word 'disease.'

This interpretative community is becoming further ambient with the prevalence of digital technology most notably, (social media) and journalists' inter-validation both within and beyond the journalistic field. The Twitterized community of China correspondents echoes Boczkowski's (2010) argument of technology intensifying imitation among journalists.

As repeatedly emphasized throughout this chapter, positional pressure is the key for understanding any routine practice or journalistic logic. News organizations with more economic and symbolic capital occupy a much more autonomous position, and this advantage of organizational position can transfer to individual journalists. Such journalists often lead, rather than follow, the tribe. News organizations' autonomy also enables them to take a more aggressive or transforming strategy in negotiating with external pressures. This is what Bourdieu (2005) says about powerful agents in the field 'distort[ing] the whole space.' But in the case of *The New York Times*, Bloomberg, and *The Wall Street Journal*'s collective coverage on China's top official corruption in 2012, though these leading agents' practice shook up the Chinese authorities and appeared to be transforming the power relations between them, the ensuing coercion by the Chinese government largely silenced the distortive forces of these powerful agents. The field of foreign correspondence in China is, thus, overall heteronomous rather than autonomous.

However, ironically, China is constantly blaming foreign media's China coverage for being 'biased' and 'hostile,' meaning the existing power structure of the field of China correspondence is, to say the least, not in the interest of China. Yet the efforts taken by Chinese authorities to constrain accessible sources, especially expert sources, are in effect helping to reproduce and reinforce the existing power structure of the field. As Hannerz (2004) notes, the bonding of the tribe is likely to be closer especially in tough places where they are 'in an adversarial or at least closely guarded relationship with the host society and especially its government' (p. 157). A further bonding journalistic community intensifies both local and durational modes of collective interpretation (Zelizer, 1993). More evidence of China's censoring practice which results in reproducing the existing power structure is to be presented and discussed in Chapter 6.

Last but not least, though collective reference risks the sin of pack journalism, this chapter cautions against rushing to an equation between the two concepts, as the former is a journalistic professional necessity due to positional pressure in the journalistic field, whereas the latter, as in its widely employed critical connotation, is the negative yet unnecessary result of the former.

Notes

1 Similar analysis and critiques on 'pack journalism' are seen in Crouse (1973), Frank (2003), Herman and Chomsky (1988), Pedelty (1995), McCluskey (2008), and Sigal (1973).
2 Personal communication, April, 2016.
3 Page, J., Spegele, B. & Eder, S. (April 7, 2012). 'Jackie Kennedy of China' at center of political drama. *The Wall Street Journal*. Retrieved from https://www.wsj.com/articles/SB10001424052702303299604577327472813686432
4 Barboza, D. (October 5, 2012). Billions in hidden riches for family of Chinese leader. *The New York Times*, Retrieved from http://www.nytimes.com/2012/10/26/business/global/family-of-wen-jiabao-holds-a-hidden-fortune-in-china.html
5 Forsythe's story on Xi Jinping's family fortune was published on June 29, 2012, but the original accessible article was later made only available to subscribers in 2017; in 2018, the whole series was removed from Bloomberg online archive with no explanation.
6 Personal communication, April, 2016.
7 The story never appeared on Bloomberg, and its leading journalist for the piece, Michael Forsythe, later joined *The New York Times*, where he published a similar piece in 2015: www.nytimes.com/2015/04/29/world/asia/wang-jianlin-abillionaire-at-the-intersection-of-business-and-power-in-china.html?smid=tw-share&_r=1
8 Krishnan's article on the survey can be retrieved here: http://indiatoday.intoday.in/story/chinese-internet-users-prefer-pak-to-india-as-neighbour-says-survey/1/571436.html
9 The Foreign Ministry started regular weekly press briefings beginning in 1982. The frequency of press briefings was changed to twice a week in 1995, and later changed to daily in 2011.
10 Denyer, S. (April 14, 2017). Chocolate cake and chemistry repair U.S.-China ties. But will North Korea spoil the party? *The Washington Post*. Retrieved from https://www.washingtonpost.com/world/chocolate-cake-and-chemistry-repair-us-china-ties-but-will-north-korea-spoil-the-party/2017/04/14/5cf5a950-206e-11e7-bb59-a74ccaf1d02f_story.html?

11 MacLeod, C. (June 20, 2017). China's pursuit of artificial intelligence worries America. *The Times*.
12 Anderlini, J. (May 26, 2014). China clamps down on US consulting groups. *Financial Times*. Retrieved from www.ft.com/content/310d29ea-e263-11e3-89fd-00144feabdc0
13 See Bill Bishop's blog introduction at https://sinocism.com/about-2/
14 The six compounds are Sanlitun Diplomatic Compound, Jianguomen Outer Diplomatic Compound, Qijiayuan Diplomatic Compound, Liangmaqiao Diplomatic Compound, Tayuan Diplomatic Compound, and Jindao Diplomatic Compound.
15 Examples of the events involving China correspondents: http://beijingbookworm.com/happenings/introducing-the-china-10-journalism-panel/
16 Personal communication, August, 2017.
17 Hernández, J. (August 17, 2017). Chinese video on border standoff with India provokes accusations of racism. *The New York Times*. Retrieved from https://www.nytimes.com/2017/08/17/world/asia/china-india-racist-video-border-standoff.html?_r=0
18 BBC. (August 17, 2017). Chinese media 'racist' video on India clash sparks anger. Retrieved from http://www.bbc.com/news/world-asia-china-40957719
19 Feng, E. & Kazmin, A. (August 17, 2017). Chinese video mocks India over Himalayas border stand-off. *Financial Times*. Retrieved from https://www.ft.com/content/0dbfbb60-8300-11e7-a4ce-15b2513cb3ff
20 DeGrandpre, A. (August 17, 2017). Chinese state media made a racist video about India and is censoring its critics. *The Washington Post*. Retrieved from https://www.washingtonpost.com/news/worldviews/wp/2017/08/17/chinese-state-media-made-a-racist-video-about-india-and-is-censoring-its-critics/?utm_term=.9de417253240
21 Joanna Chiu's personal website keeps a detailed record of her media commentaries: https://joannachiu.com/essays-and-columns/
22 Grigg, A. & Murray, L. (March 24, 2016). The cult of Xi Jinping. *Australian Financial Review*. Pg. 24; The ChinaFile conversation is retrieved from http://www.chinafile.com/conversation/xi-jinping-cult-personality
23 Personal communication, February, 2016.
24 China correspondents are asked in the survey to name which news organization takes the lead if they think a hierarchy exists in the field of China reporting. Of all 101 respondents, only 36 provided their answer, and two disagree on the notion of hierarchy in foreign press corps in China. Of the 34 responses acknowledging the existence of a hierarchy, the most mentioned is *The New York Times* ($N = 24$), followed by Reuters ($N = 17$), *The Wall Street Journal* ($N = 12$), and BBC ($N = 10$).
25 In the survey, one question asks respondents to rate the perceived impact of 'other China correspondents' on their daily reporting work on a five-point scale. Significant cross-national variance is found: $F(3,97) = 5.09$, $p = .003$. A Tukey HSD post hoc test further suggests that correspondents from Democratic Corporatist countries perceive significantly higher influence from other China correspondents ($M = 3.00$) compared with those from Polarized Pluralist ($M = 2.22$) and non-Western countries ($M = 2.00$).
26 The three mainstream Japanese newspapers (English-language version) are *Japan News*, *Asia & Japan Watch* (*AJW*) and *the Mainichi*. The finding is based on a search on Factiva.
27 Goldkorn, J. (March 16, 2017). Chris Buckley: The China journalist's China journalist. Retrieved from https://supchina.com/podcast/chris-buckley-china-journalists-china-journalist/

6 'The anaconda in the chandelier'

China's uncodified state coercion

In previous chapters, I have briefly tapped on the distinctively rigorous press control in China. As a repressive practice imposed by the authorities on information producers, state coercion or censorship on media entails an eternal tug of war with the concepts of press freedom and the rights to know, yet a 'structural necessity' in the field of symbolic production (Bourdieu, 1994). In exerting pressures on foreign press, China is known for long embracing the most sophisticated and omnidirectional coercive strategies, ranging from surveillance by means of the infamous massive internet censorship project 'Great Firewall' to old-fashioned physical harassment and assault on journalists and their sources, and what Herman and Chomsky (1988) call 'flak.'

These uncodified coercive practices, without explicit reference to laws and regulations, are institutionalized into a consensual confrontation between the political pressure from China and foreign press corps who are reluctantly well informed about the censorship they would face. Perry Link (2002) names this uncodified coercion or censorship of China as 'the anaconda in the chandelier': a hidden devil with devastating power, and the devastating power lies more in people's fear or anticipation than its real damage. This metaphor parallels what Lee (2000) calls 'imagined external pressure,' which can be more intimidating than the real pressures because of the ambiguousness and uncertainty. The uncertainty associated with these uncodified coercive practices tends to lead journalists to take countermeasures to circumvent and negotiate with the interventions. Self-censorship is one of such reactions (Chalaby, 2000).

This chapter examines the external pressures on China correspondents from such looming 'anaconda' and how journalists perceive and negotiate with the disruptive pressures. It has to be noted that China's control over foreign media is sophisticated and pervasive, encompassing both explicitly codified rules and regulations and uncodified coercive strategies. Chapter 2 discussed the boundaries of the field of China correspondence set by codified rules and regulations; the focus of this chapter is on uncodified state coercion.

State coercion as heteronomous power

State intervention in media is a major heteronomous power influencing the journalistic field. In democracies, state intervention is mainly realized through ownership, funding, and regulations (Hallin & Mancini, 2004), but in authoritarian states 'an elaborate system of censorship and coercion' is institutionalized in an effort to control the media (Lee, 2001). No matter in what form, such intervention is the power struggle between the journalistic field and its immediate and larger political field, and 'one important task then for a generalizable theory of journalistic-political field relations is to classify and analyze the various forms of state coercive power over the media' (Benson, 2005, p. 93).

Coercive power can be exerted through both reward and punishment (Lee, 1998), as well as through what Bourdieu calls 'symbolic violence,' a process of hegemony that is accepted by the dominated as assumed de facto, which can be translated into unconscious self-censorship. Hassid (2008) in his study on China's control over domestic media proposes the notion of 'regime of uncertainty,' referring to the Chinese government using an uncodified set of media control mechanisms to effectively coerce Chinese journalists into practicing self-censorship. Pedelty (1995) also notes that feelings of disorientation make foreign correspondents more vulnerable to the propaganda of the host country. Thus, uncodified coercion, with the looming of its perceived or 'imagined pressures,' is more likely to incite journalists' self-censorship (Lee, 2001). This is a typical result of the negotiation between agents and institutional pressure, or between the journalistic field and the political field. Journalistic autonomy is compromised trading for individual agents' positions to be unchallenged and capital not undermined.

Coercing foreign correspondents in China

Major foreign news organizations and correspondents, including their news assistants, are closely monitored and coerced in an effort to minimize their 'unfavourable' coverage on China. Such coercive measures targeting foreign correspondents include both carrot and stick. 'Stick' may include interrogation, physical assault, physical and digital surveillance, denying or threatening to deny reporters' visas, restricting reporters' information access, and harassment of sources and news assistants. 'Carrot,' on the contrary, ranges from honour, scoops offered, and exclusive interviews to access to government officials (Lee, 1998), sometimes also buy-off.

Based on interviews with China correspondents and the abundant accounts of China correspondents' experience with Chinese coercion, I categorize the most commonly used strategies of coercion as harassment, direct access blockage, flak, and reward.

Harassment

State-initiated harassment on foreign correspondents' reporting activities is seen in many countries. As documented in previous studies, foreign correspondents based in South Africa, Singapore, Russia, and Latin America all reported having been contained or harassed in similar, rather than different, ways (see e.g. Hannerz, 2004; Waisbord, 2002).

Harassment as a repressive social control in non-democratic regimes includes surveillance, low-intensity physical harassment, and intimidation (Gerschewski, 2013; Pearce, 2015). It is the most common daily state-initiated coercive practice foreign correspondents have to face in China. Previous studies suggest that the level of government-initiated harassment against the media and journalists is correlated with the threats the governments perceive and the contrary ideological positions the governments, especially the top leaders, hold (see e.g. Kellam & Stein, 2016; VonDoepp & Young, 2012). Following this vein, we can assume that in an increasingly totalitarian China upholding Leninist press theory, harassment against foreign media and journalists, especially those from liberal Western countries, is more intense.

Foreign Correspondents Club China (FCCC) reports in 2015 that 72% of the surveyed foreign correspondents have self-reportedly experienced interference or obstruction during reporting activities, including being 'shoved roughly and repeatedly,' having reporting equipment snatched away, and being pointed at by assault rifles and shotguns (FCCC, 2015).

Former China correspondent for Al Jazeera English Melissa Chan, who saw her Press Card discontinued by MOFA in 2012, recounts that 'local officials or thugs' are the main direct source of harassment (Chan, 2017). The thugs, hired by local authority, serve as 'proxy amateur police,' and the officials would offer to assist, only to frustrate journalists in bureaucratic red tape aimed at delaying the reporting activities – 'an effective ploy for any news team on deadline' (Chan, 2017).

Delaying tactics are widely used and work effectively for obstructing time-sensitive reporting work. NPR Beijing correspondent Anthony Kuhn said that for most of the harassment that happens to him, local authorities are 'just wasting my time and trying to stop me from doing my job.'

The degree of harassment can be accelerated to physical confrontation, confiscation of recording equipment, and even detention and death threat.

Bernhand Zand of German magazine *Der Spiegel* recalls that on his last day of a field reporting in Guiyang, a provincial capital city in southwest China, where he was working on an investigative story about the death of five street children in a neighbouring city, their hotel room was broken into and recording digital equipment was destroyed. The incident happened only months into Zand's stint in China, and he sarcastically laughs it off: 'It's good to know from the beginning the relation with the state here.' Canadian correspondent Nathan VanderKlippe of *The Globe and Mail* travelled to Elishku in Xinjiang in August 2017 and was briefly detained by local authorities before he could even start to work. His laptop was seized and held momentarily (VanderKlippe, 2017). In the case of Bloomberg's and *New York Times*' investigative stories on China's elite politics, the leading correspondents Michael Forsythe and David Barboza were respectively threatened to leave China. Forsythe received a death threat, which was passed via informal personal communication;[1] Barboza had been threatened and stalked to the extent that he finally had to flee China.[2]

Foreign correspondents' online activities and phones are closely monitored by officials, or at least this is what many correspondents perceive to be happening. FCCC's report (2016) shows as many as 89% of the surveyed correspondents are concerned about the privacy and safety of communicating online. *The New York Times* reported that since 2008, 'Chinese hackers began targeting American news organizations as part of an effort to monitor coverage of Chinese issues' (Perlroth, 2013). The low response rate of the online survey of this study adds evidence of how foreign correspondents distrust online safety. Some correspondents asked for a hardcopy of the survey to fill out, as they deem online survey highly risky. Barboza, for example, explained to me that he was confident that his email exchange is monitored so he could not complete the survey online.[3]

On most daily occasions, harassment takes the form of *uncovered* surveillance, which is deliberately made known to the targeted correspondents as a warning of the 'hidden anaconda.' Several correspondents I talked to had similar experiences, that during reporting trips checking into a hotel room is always followed by police interrogation at the door. 'Just to tell us: we know you are here so you'd better behave,' a correspondent with a European news agency explains.[4] A German correspondent recalls that when he was applying for residency with local police, he was shocked at the police's revelation that they knew almost every person he met, even for personal reasons, in the brief period since he arrived in China.[5] An FCCC report on China correspondents' working condition in 2017 cites a journalist being summoned for coffee with State Security officials before one reporting trip and was told that the State Security knew about the journalist's reporting plans, though no intervention followed (FCCC, 2018).

Harassment of foreign press corps in China is institutional, not only targeting foreign correspondents but also going the extra length to annoy their sources and news assistants, as the reach of Chinese government to constrain foreign nationals working for foreign media is rather limited compared to coercing its own nationals. An Indian correspondent recounts an 'unbelievable' harassment his source had experienced. On a reporting trip in Ningxia, a Muslim autonomous region in northwest China, he was interviewing people about the carpet business in that region. His source, a carpet businessman, was interrogated and threatened by six local policemen after the correspondent visited him. 'Please don't write the story; please don't name me,' the businessman pleaded to the correspondent, apparently scared.[6] In rare cases, news sources are being imprisoned on charges such as 'subversion' and 'picking quarrels and provoking troubles.'[7] FCCC (2018) reports that 26% of the 117 China correspondents it surveyed have had their sources harassed, detained, or interrogated.

Chinese news assistants are easier targets of institutional harassment. FCCC (2016) reports that 33% of foreign correspondents said their news assistants had been harassed by Chinese officials in 2015. Chinese news assistants with Western news outlets are from time to time summoned for 'meeting' or 'dinner' with officials, who would ask them to spy on their foreign colleagues or simply lecture them to be 'patriotic.'[8] In extreme cases, news assistants are detained.[9]

Blocking access

China applies a strict licensing system and limited press release to control foreign press' information access; besides, it also employs uncodified coercion to block or restrict foreign correspondents' information access. One of the mechanisms is the world's largest and the most sophisticated internet filtering system, 'Golden Shield Project.' The mammoth project monitors and censors online information using bandwidth throttling, keyword filtering, blocking entire websites, and 'hand censoring' – manual efforts to remove 'improper content' (King, Pan & Roberts, 2013). It also blocks certain entire websites from being accessible in China.[10]

Besides a technical censoring effort to control online information access, China restricts foreign correspondents' access into certain regions which are deemed sensitive, though there is no law or regulation explicitly forbidding foreign journalists from entering and reporting these regions.

Due to historical, ethnical, and religious reasons, Tibet and Xinjiang, two highly unstable regions, are, in the words of David Shambaugh (2016), China's 'volatile periphery,' where clashes and unrest are not rare. The Chinese government has been trying to keep these volatile regions under control, by employing, apart from economic incentives, heavy surveillance and 'heavy-handed coercion by paramilitary forces' (Shambaugh, 2016).

These two ethnic minority–populated autonomous regions, especially Tibet, are in effect off limits to foreign correspondents. The border with North Korea is also strictly controlled. Since 2007, foreign journalists have been required to obtain prior permission for entering Tibet.[11] The restrictions grew tense after the deadly unrest in March 2008. In practice, only a scarce number of selected correspondents are allowed into Tibet in strictly organized reporting trips. An FCCC survey shows that in 2015 only one out of 142 surveyed journalists was approved for an individual reporting trip to Tibet.[12] China's Ambassador to the US Cui Tiankai recently, in an interview with NPR, explained that foreign press is not allowed into Tibet because of the high altitude of the region.[13]

Each year, China's Foreign Ministry organizes several reporting trips to various regions of China, occasionally including Tibet. In November 2015, 14 foreign journalists went on an organized reporting trip to Tibet.[14] For foreign correspondents, it would be the only channel to get a glimpse into the region, though a highly manipulated glimpse. But usually the notice is issued only around 10 days before the trip, or with even shorter notice, catching journalists unprepared. The selection process is also obscure. For the 2015 reporting trip, the invitation notice posted on the Foreign Ministry's website reads, 'The IPC (International Press Center) will determine the final list of participants in an appropriate way.'[15] But this 'appropriate way' of selection is never made known to the journalists. A German correspondent complains, 'It's not transparent. They will not tell you why you are qualified or not qualified.'[16]

During such trips, schedule and reporting activities are carefully arranged and strictly limited. Journalists are required to stay with the group throughout the trip and not allowed to exit halfway.[17] Journalists who have joined such reporting trips complain there were 'no opportunities for independent reporting.' Australian correspondent Angus Grigg, who was on the 2016 reporting trip to Tibet, describes the whole trip as 'a propaganda war' (Grigg, 2016).

Compared to Tibet, Xinjiang is more accessible to foreign press. Official permission is not a requirement. But provincial-level coercion manages to keep certain parts of the region effectively inaccessible for foreign press, as in the aforementioned case of Canadian journalist VanderKlippe. The situation is reported to have deteriorated noticeably since 2018, when China's mass surveillance and detention targeting on ethnic Uighurs in the region scaled up. The latest survey by FCCC (2019) in 2018 shows that 89% of those China correspondents who travelled to Xinjiang experienced restriction and harassment by local officials and security agents. Bloomberg journalist Peter Martin was greeted by four armed policemen on his arrival to the city of Khorgas in Xinjiang, and was ordered to kneel on the ground for a thorough inspection (Martin, 2019).

Flak: 'hostile foreign forces'

Herman and Chomsky (1988), in their seminal book *Manufacturing Consent*, define flak as one of the 'filters' employed by money and power to control the media, 'negative responses to a media statement or a program' in order to discipline and discredit the media organization or reporters (p. 26). In the field of China correspondence, flak is a highly preferred coercive strategy the Chinese authorities employ to discredit the correspondents, hence undermining the social impact of their reports and their reporting environment on the whole.

Chinese state media and officials often accuse foreign press of 'biased reporting' by 'hostile foreign forces.' Flak usually is used at the end of the newsmaking process, as a post-report retaliation to generate a chilling effect among the whole foreign press corps. When used in a more general denouncing scenario (i.e., not specifically targeting an individual story or journalist), it is also deemed a long-term strategy to cultivate a perceived climate that pointed to the foreign press's hostility toward China.

Discredit individual correspondent

Accreditation and visa have been a passive-aggressive way to control, or to punish, foreign correspondents if their stories displease the authorities. Correspondents can be denied or discontinued accreditation, thus effectively being disqualified from playing in the field, though more often journalists' visa and accreditation renewals are delayed or threatened not to renew, as a serious warning.

The most recent case of discontinuing foreign correspondent's accreditation was American journalist Megha Rajagopalan. Rajagopalan has been the BuzzFeed China correspondent since 2016 and was formerly with Reuters in Beijing for four years. While reporting for BuzzFeed, she was on a temporary J2 visa valid for six months, which is becoming the norm for accrediting foreign online news media in China. After an investigative series on the highly sensitive topic of China's mass surveillance and detention targeting ethnic Uighurs in Xinjiang, her journalist visa renewal was rejected and she had to leave China unprepared. No official explanation was offered.[18]

In late 2015 when I was doing my field research in Beijing, French newsmagazine *L'Obs* China correspondent Ursula Gauthier was denied the renewal of her J1 visa (standard journalist visa valid for 12 months). Both the Foreign Ministry and state-run newspapers harshly criticized her for writing a critical article on China's policy in Xinjiang, which 'blatantly championed acts of terrorism and slaughter of innocent civilians, igniting indignation among the Chinese people'; and Foreign Ministry claims that Gauthier is 'no longer suitable to continue working in China.'[19] An earlier case of discrediting a foreign correspondent was in 2012, when Al Jazeera English China correspondent Melissa Chan's application of visa renewal was denied and she was consequently expelled. Again, no official explanation was offered. The Foreign Ministry spokesperson only vaguely addressed the issue: 'I think relevant media and journalists are clear about that' (Earp, 2012).

Except for the case of Gauthier, in most cases of expulsion, official explanation is either nonexistent or vague. Vague rhetoric here works to amplify the effectiveness of coercion, scaring journalists away from as many sensitive lines as possible.

Discrediting individual correspondents is not limited to visa and accreditation measures. Chinese state media outlets are also used to discredit the reputation of foreign correspondents by verbally attacking them for critical stories, especially those critical of Chinese top leaders. Australian correspondent Angus Grigg was singled out by Chinese state tabloid *Global Times* for 'ignoring the development and progress in Tibet' and 'distorted and biased reporting.'[20] *Wall Street Journal* Beijing correspondent Jeremy Page in March 2012 broke the story on the alleged corruption case of Bo Xilai, a high-ranking power contender, and the paper was accused of bribing Chinese officials for access to information for scoops. Dow Jones, the paper's parent company, denied the charge, and attributed the accusation to Chinese authorities' rage with Page's story on Bo (Young, 2013).

Punish news organization

More often than bashing individual correspondents, the flak targets the news organizations. Organizational flak can cause personal suffering, if the top management should decide to comply with the demand.

After the rows over the aforementioned investigative report on China's top leaders' family wealth, the Bloomberg News website has been blocked in China. The company's most lucrative business, financial information terminal service, has been banned from selling to Chinese state companies for years. All incoming correspondents' visa applications were denied. The organizational pressure finally led to an open spat with relevant journalists' professionalism claim, amid which its leading journalist Forsythe was suspended.[21] *The New York Times* experienced similar punishment for its story on the alleged corruption of the Wen Jiabao family.[22] Access to its websites and applications online remains blocked at the time of this writing.

The Guardian, BBC, *The Economist*, Reuters, and Japan's *Yomiuri Shimbun* are also among the foreign news outlets that have had their websites partially or fully blocked according to data from GreatFire.org, a watchdog monitoring Chinese internet censorship. All Reuters's news websites, including both English-language and Chinese-language sites, have been blocked since March 2015. When asked about the reason for the censorship, a senior editor of Reuters said, 'Yes, we know the specific reason. But I probably cannot share that with you. Let's just simply say it's about a story they [Chinese government] are not happy with.'[23]

Traditional media censorship such as banning sales or ripping off certain pages from each copy of a newsmagazine is still a common practice. Subscribers to *The Economist* in China reported having received their copies with pages ripped out or passages blacked out by a marker.[24] BBC and CNN both have reported being blacked out in China during live broadcasting.[25]

Discredit foreign press

Apart from the case-based flak against individual journalists or news organizations as punishment, China has been long attacking foreign media, especially Western media, as if they were monolithic. As a Reuters correspondent puts it,

> People in China, for a very long time, do not trust foreign media. We are often portrayed as 'hostile forces,' as 'anti-Chinese,' which we are not. I would say the vast majority of us are not. The vast majority are here because we care about the country. Many of us love this country. But the government is very good at convincing people that we are hostile.[26]

China has traditionally been nationalistic (Townsend, 1992; Unger, 2016). Chinese society has long resisted foreign penetration, and the sentiment of nationalism has surged to new heights in recent years. Chinese government seeks to promote a more xenophobic climate among the public. School history textbooks and the entire educational system emphasize the evilness of Western imperialism and the China's history of victimhood at its hands, suffering as a result of national humiliation by foreign powers (Kaufman, 2010). A nationwide campaign against 'foreign spies' is relentlessly carried on, warning Chinese nationals to be alert of foreigners who are highly likely to be spies (Reuters, 2017).

A *Global Attitudes Survey* by the Pew Research Center in 2016 shows that 77% of the respondents surveyed in China believe 'our way of life needs to be protected against foreign influence.' Such sentiment has been stable in recent years, according to the Pew Research Center (Pew, 2016). Mass protests against Japan, America, and the Philippines have been seen in the past decade in China, with some escalating into violent clashes.[27]

The high rise of xenophobia has a direct impact on the foreign press corps, who have been experiencing suspicion and hostility from the

Chinese public. In 2017, three Japanese journalists, while reporting on an explosion at a kindergarten in East China, were attacked by local Chinese who were shouting 'down with the Japanese imperialists!' and their Chinese employees were called 'Chinese traitor' and 'Japanese spy' (FCCC, 2018).

The hostility was especially escalated after a Tibet riot in March 2008, when Tibetans and Han Chinese clashed, resulting in hundreds of casualties. Mainstream Western media, who were then allowed to enter Tibet, largely reported that Chinese police used excessive force, which was contradictory to the official narrative in Chinese media. After acting swiftly to impose bans on foreign media's access to Tibet, China launched mass campaigns accusing Western media of being biased. College students organized an 'anti-CNN' campaign to condemn its reports as 'the lies and distortions of facts.'[28] Their activities were supported by state media with considerable coverage, which agitated another nationwide wave of sentiment against Western media. There was even a rap video singing 'Don't be too CNN,' which soon became a hit in China's cyber world.[29]

Efforts to discredit foreign media never cease, with Chinese state-owned news media playing a significant role. The *Global Times*, a jingoistic tabloid owned by the Party's mouthpiece *People's Daily*, is at the forefront of such endeavour, constantly branding Western media as 'bad-mouthing' China,[30] 'distorting the history' and 'smearing China.'[31] Even young rappers bash in English for the 'prejudices fabricated by foreign media' (Li, 2016).

Foreign correspondents, especially those who are not ethnic Chinese and thus are easily identifiable, are most likely to encounter suspicion and obstruction on a daily basis (Farmer, 1990). They are almost destined to be labelled 'foreign hostile forces' as part of the Western conspiracy to contain China's rise (Allen-Ebrahimian, 2016). When NPR correspondent Frank Langfitt was researching for a story on a bridge collapse incident in a small town, the mother of his interviewee repeatedly told her son not to speak to Langfitt because she was convinced that he was aiming to 'malign China and the Communist Party' (Langfitt, 2017).

Currying reward

Coercive strategies are by no means confined to only punishment. Similar to what Lee (1998) notes on how Beijing co-opted Hong Kong media, China has developed a sophisticated set of co-optative mechanisms to tame foreign press, by means of gifts, throwing banquets, and favouring pro-China journalists with scoops, exclusive interviews, and access to government officials.

On the eve of Xi Jinping's state visit to the UK in 2015, Reuters was granted an exclusive interview with Xi.[32] Likewise, *The Wall Street Journal* got the exclusive interview later in the same year before Xi set off for a visit to the US.[33] Meanwhile, as some are awarded, others are deliberately left out. At the unveiling of the new Politburo Standing Committee that Xi Jinping hand-picked for his second term in office, *Financial Times*, among others, was excluded. Its Beijing bureau chief Tom Mitchell thinks it was because of some critical columns they published: 'It was never said so explicitly, but ever since those columns came out, there have been a few examples of us just not being invited to things that other people have been invited to' (FCCC, 2018).

Negotiating with coercive pressures

When being asked to rate the extent to which the regime's efforts at *harassment* and *access blockage* influenced their work, China correspondents from various national contexts rated access blockage much more disruptive than harassment.[34] Harassment is invariably perceived with mild influence, contrary to the notion that correspondents from liberal Western countries are more subject to government-initiated harassment. This discrepancy is to be interpreted by addressing journalists' negotiation with these coercive pressures.

Rather than choosing a frontal battle to fight back, China correspondents tend to develop a set of 'anticipatory avoidance mechanisms' (Gans, 1979), whereby they anticipate possible forms of pressure and take measures to circumvent them.

Anticipatory avoidance

As press censorship in China has become a familiar narrative in the community of China correspondents, they generally have prepared for the potential harassment and retaliation and have knowledge about which 'taboo topics' could invite trouble. A *Wall Street Journal* correspondent observes, 'I think the Chinese government is following the Singapore model. You can be here, but don't get much into Singaporean politics. There's severe penalty if you do: fines, bans, expulsion, prosecutions.'[35]

China correspondents have reportedly developed strategies of routines to avoid harassment. They are quick in spotting a plainclothes policeman tailing them. They know staying in a car for the night is safer than checking into a local hotel. They speed up interviews and disappear before local authorities are alarmed. They avoid talking over the phone or exchanging emails over topics that might irritate the Chinese government. They usually choose to follow officials' directives, hoping that their passports are not taken away for 'checking.' An AFP correspondent is annoyed by the check-your-visa excuse as a way to detain journalists for hours: 'This is the moment you have to leave [the spot], or maybe just hide away for a while.'[36]

When Australian correspondent Angus Grigg joined an organized reporting trip to Tibet, he had anticipated that the whole arrangement would be staged. With other journalists, he snuck out in a taxi driving towards a monastery, which the local officials tried to prevent them from visiting. When they saw another car tailing them, as expected, they aptly changed cars, played hide-and-seek, 'like any well-trained operative in the movies' (Grigg, 2016).

China correspondents, especially those from Anglo-American news organizations, are more discreet about the professional routines in news reporting: balance, fairness, and objectivity, which, as discussed in Chapter 4, protect them from attacks. A journalist with *The New York Times* comments, 'Those stories need to be accurate [to avoid being picked on]. . . . We're dealing with a very powerful government [in China]. . . . We would be very careful and fair.'[37]

Fighting back

Only sporadically do foreign correspondents stage a frontal fight with censors. This fight can take place at both individual and organizational levels, though often journalists are frustrated when their employers choose to concede to China's censorship demands.

You harass; I record

For journalists, the most convenient and powerful weapon to fight against state coercion is via the tricks of their trade: to record the incident of harassment and make it into news, or as Waisbord (2002) calls it, 'deterrence by publicity.' A dramatic case of harassing journalists could hype up the original story and enrich its salience in the news pool. This is called by Gans (1979) the 'heating effect,' in contrast to the 'chilling effect' which aims to muzzle the press.

Take the case of Australian correspondent Grigg on the Tibet reporting trip. He failed to visit the monastery in the end, but he recorded the whole adventure in a story that revealed the intrigues of police scrutiny:

> On the road out of town, a taxi drew level with our car, slowed down, looked in through the windows, then sped off. Just to be sure, it allowed us to overtake a few kilometres down the road, which permitted them another look.
>
> Then came the road block. On the turn-off to the monastery, police had erected a checkpoint just for us. We were stopped and, after being

forcefully told the monastery was closed, were sent back to town with an escort.

(Grigg, 2016)

Similarly, Nathan VanderKlippe of *The Globe and Mail* wrote down his experience of being briefly detained in Xinjiang and published an account of roughly 2,000 words in his paper.[38] VanderKlippe also live tweeted the whole incident in several Twitter posts, which soon entered the news arena even before his paper covered it. News outlets including the *Huff-Post* reported the incident, based on VanderKlippe's tweets.[39] Global journalists' associations and organizations, including Committee to Protect Journalists, Reporters Without Borders, and International Federation of Journalists issued notice condemning the incident.[40]

Broadcasting media are taking advantage of sound and visuals, which are more effective in hyping up stories on authority harassment of journalists. In November 2016, BBC Shanghai correspondent John Sudworth tried to interview an independent candidate for a local level election at the candidate's home in the outskirts of Beijing, only to find himself shoved and his interviews terminated by a group of unidentified local men. Video footage[41] from BBC shows that more than 10 men in plainclothes stood as a human shield in front of the door of the candidate's home, preventing the candidate from even opening her own door, before the police gathered in larger numbers and got aggressive, forcing the BBC reporting team out. 'So this is democracy of Chinese style: a large group of thugs are pushing us away . . . the woman inside hoping to stand for the election won't be able to do the interview,' Sudworth explains in the video, with the scene of him being shoved away. The video soon exploded online and was escalated into the narrative of 'China's censoring of the press' and 'Chinese fake democracy.' On YouTube alone, the clip attracted more than 115,000 views; on Facebook it hit 69,742 shares and more than 6,600,000 views.[42]

Similarly, Sun (2015), in her study of foreign correspondents as 'antagonistic' to China's public diplomacy efforts, also points out that 'incidents of foreign correspondents' expulsion from China themselves become newsworthy.' This 'foreign correspondent versus an oppressive regime' narrative has its long-lasting appeal.

Organizational fight and home state intervene

Journalists, when confronted with external pressure on their journalistic work, would first turn to their news organizations for support, who would negotiate terms with the Chinese government. But journalists do not always benefit from strong institutional support. In the case of Melissa Chan's expulsion, Al Jazeera headquarters explained the incident as an 'accident,' saying it could have been avoided should the bureau and the management lobby in a more efficient way.[43]

In some extreme cases, the home government gets involved in the negotiation process. When a *Washington Post* reporter was expelled for reporting a sensitive story, the paper's executives reportedly invited the Chinese ambassador to the US for tea and asked Henry Kissinger to bring the case to the then vice premier of China (Pen America, 2016). Other management raised the issue with the visiting president Jiang Zemin during an interview session with him. After all these efforts, the expelled correspondent found his way back to China.

Having exposed the alleged corruption and family wealth of Chinese leaders, nine *New York Times* journalists and 14 Bloomberg journalists faced the similar situation of having their visas discontinued (Nakamura & Wan, 2013). The US government made several public efforts to intervene. Vice President Joseph Biden raised the issue in his meeting with Xi Jinping, harshly warning of 'consequences for China if they proceeded to oust the reporters' (Shear, 2014). After Biden's public effort, China restored accreditations to some, though not all, of the journalists involved.

Foreign press corps are divided on whether state intervention should be evoked in dealing with strict censorship in China, especially to lessen harassment and flak. In 2012, 26 German correspondents in China wrote to German Chancellor Merkel asking her to intervene on their behalf to stop the harassment they have been experiencing.[44] But several American correspondents interviewed expressed disapproval of asking for government intervention on grounds of 'independent press.' One of them makes a straightforward statement: 'I don't think US government should get involved in any kind of media policy at all.'

Surrender

Worn out by unsuccessful fighting back, foreign correspondents do sometimes surrender to pressure. When asked if he would file a complaint to Foreign Ministry or FCCC for reporting activities disrupted, an American correspondent replied in a cavalier tone, 'No. Filing a complaint will not help us. It will just take us more time and won't get any results.' It's worth noting that the correspondent himself is a member of the FCCC Media Freedom Committee, which fights against harassment and surveillance targeting foreign press corps in China.

For access blockage, correspondents, mostly constrained by pressing deadlines and limited resources, would give up pushing for an undefinable grey zone and drop certain stories. In the case of Xinjiang, Julie Makinen of the *Los Angeles Times* says difficulty in gaining access to that region has led to a decrease in coverage of the area after 2014, according to PEN

America's report. For organized reporting trips to Tibet, many foreign correspondents do not make the effort to apply for permission, saying they either believe they would not be granted one or regard the organized trip as being too limited for any journalistic purpose (PEN America, 2016).

Serious threat or witnessing such threat does prevent correspondents from working on certain sensitive topics. As recorded in PEN's report, American correspondent Paul Mooney decided to drop a story on a mass protest in Beijing in 2011, where 'a dozen journalists' were assaulted by security officers. 'It was really scary,' Mooney told PEN America. 'To see this, I myself became afraid. I told myself there were no real protesters, no news, nothing to write about. Maybe I justified to myself that there was no story' (PEN America, 2016, p. 18).

More often, foreign correspondents give in to such censorship for the safety concern of sources. The Indian correspondent, after his source for a story on a carpet business in a Muslim autonomous region was harassed, decided to give up the story, but 'can't help thinking where is a safe zone for China story.'[45]

Built-in anticipatory avoidance: self-censorship

A large number of the above cases of negotiating with censorship are in effect voluntary acts journalists take to ward off foreseeable coercion by Chinese authorities. Over time, journalists have developed a set of 'built-in anticipatory avoidance mechanisms' (Gans, 1979, p. 276). Self-censorship is a set of editorial actions 'in anticipation of currying reward and avoiding punishments from the power structure' (Lee, 1998, p. 57), a powerful and insidious form of censorship, the unrecognized submission to the power structure. It is a voluntary practice of censorship by the information producer on his/her own symbolic work in order to avoid external censorship, seen as a compromise between expressive interest and social forces (Bourdieu, 1991; Brownlie, 2014; Gans, 1979; etc.).

Journalists would resist the term 'self-censorship,' as in lay usage it suggests a conscious self-censorship giving in of journalistic autonomy to the heteronomous powers. However, in practice, self-censorship is most often exercised unconsciously. As Lee (1998) notes, there is a 'third-person effect' in journalists' perceiving external pressures on editorial autonomy: journalists usually downplay their own tendency of self-censorship but see their colleagues more prone to practices of self-censorship. As censorship is a 'structural necessity' (Bourdieu, 1994), so is self-censorship.

Extreme cases of censorship, such as expelling a correspondent for an uncharged crime, do intensify the tendency toward self-censorship among foreign press corps, to a certain extent. In commenting on the expelled French correspondent Ursula Gauthier, a Colombian correspondent emphasized the notion of 'limitation' several times: 'I know the *limitation* . . . I think once you know you work in a state with censorship, it's better to work within the *limitation* . . . I've chosen to work within *limitations*.' A German correspondent foresees no such risk for himself, because 'I don't touch those topics.'

But for other journalists, extreme censorship may produce an opposite effect, especially when censorship itself is a perfect fit for the 'authoritarian China' narrative in international news discourse. In the case of Gauthier's expulsion, *The Guardian* alone ran seven stories (including one editorial), criticizing China's 'crackdown on foreign media,' maintaining that 'any attempt to impose self-censorship on the foreign press in China should be strongly resisted.'[46] Again, such a 'chilling effect' may end up as a 'heating effect,' adding to embarrassment for the Chinese authorities, working contrary to their expectations.

Conclusion

This chapter looks at state coercion as a major source of external pressure on the field of foreign correspondence and how journalists negotiate with these pressures. Chinese authorities use both 'carrot and stick' to tame foreign press to its own interest. Harassment, access blockage, and flak are widely used 'sticks.' In addition to being denied access to certain areas and information channels, China correspondents report being under both online and offline surveillance, physical harassment, and intimidation.

Between harassment and access blockage, China correspondents unanimously perceive much more influence from the latter, though anecdotally harassment is a major source of external pressure on China correspondents' news production. Correspondents from Anglo-American countries do not report significantly higher pressure from harassment, though they are assumed to experience more cases of state-initiated harassment in China. These discrepancies are to be interpreted by addressing the journalists' negotiation with coercive pressures.

With harassment, China correspondents negotiate using a set of 'anticipatory avoidance mechanisms' to circumvent or downplay these manufactured obstacles. Compared with harassment, little room is allowed to negotiate with access blockage. But access blockage does not necessarily lead the journalists to entirely drop the topic. Instead, journalists may negotiate with such pressure by means of exposing censorship and turning to other available but one-sided sources. Thus, these coercive measures often fail to tame the field of China correspondence. For example, on the off-limit topic of Tibet, foreign correspondents admit that 'a lack of access to Tibet increases their reliance on exile sources and overseas academics, who may have particular agenda and lack up-to-date information' (FCCC, 2016).

The same unsuccessful attempt is the practice of using flak to retaliate against individual correspondents and their news organizations, as well as to deliver a chilling effect among foreign press corps. As the foreign press corps is not monolithic, they respond to censorship with varying strategies. A more conscious self-censorship, as expected by the censors, is not guaranteed. On the contrary, flak itself is most likely to find its way into the news narrative. In the same vein, excessive harassment may result in a 'heating effect.' Mild harassment, on the other hand, could have its censorship effect compromised, with journalists aptly adopting anticipatory avoidance mechanisms.

Amid the massive-scaled omnipresent state coercion by China, foreign correspondents often find themselves struggling in a difficult situation, as the political power from China is supported by and intertwined with power from other fields, such as economic field. Jocelyn Ford, former Beijing bureau chief for *Marketplace*, describes the situation as, 'How do you fight against a bully is the question – a rich bully' (PEN America, 2016, p. 33). The rich bully here is a powerful state player meshing both political and economic coercion, promising tense power struggles between the journalistic field on its own logic and the external pressures exerted by this rich bully. Foreign news organizations have to carefully balance journalistic autonomy and the chance of not being able to report from China, and also financial consequences should they be barred from China which to them is both an attractive news beat and a lucrative market, especially for the financial media. For non-commercial news organizations, financial loss may not be a big concern, but neither are they exempt from a tug of war in the field, as they face the same political coercion, to say the least.

This chapter explores the increasingly aggressive state coercion in China as a major disruptive external force and attempts to present how China correspondents negotiate with such pervasive heteronomous power. The field of China correspondence, though functioning on its own journalistic logic, is heavily subjected to heteronomous pressures from state coercion in the host country of China. Although foreign correspondents take countermeasures, including exposing harassment and anticipatory avoidance, none of these measures addresses the structural conditions. The power structure is hardly challenged, with the 'anaconda in the chandelier' continuing to be writhing in the field and threatening the journalistic practice of China correspondents.

Notes

1 Personal communication, January, 2016.
2 PEN America. (2016). Darkened Screen: constraints on foreign journalists in China. Retrieved from https://pen.org/sites/default/files/PEN_foreign_journalists_ report_FINAL_online%5B1%5D.pdf

3 Email exchange with David Barboza from the end of 2015 to January 2016.

4 Personal communication, February, 2016.

5 Personal communication, February, 2016.

6 Personal communication, February, 2016.

7 A Tibetan activist was sentenced to five years in prison on charge of 'inciting separatism' after *The New York Times* interviewed him. See www.nytimes.com/2018/05/22/world/asia/tibetan-activist-tashi-wangchuk-sentenced.html

8 Personal communication with several Chinese news assistants; also see PEN America report, p. 30.

9 In 2014, the news assistant to German journalist Angela Köckritz of *Die Zeit* was detained for nine months for helping Köckritz report on Hong Kong's pro-democracy movement in October 2014.

10 *New York Times*, Reuters, BBC, and Hong Kong-based *South China Morning Post* are among the news outlets having their websites blocked in China. See Tai, Z. (2010). Casting the ubiquitous net of information control: Internet surveillance in China from golden shield to green dam. *International Journal of Advanced Pervasive and Ubiquitous Computing (IJAPUC)*, *2*(1), 53–70.

11 According to International Press Center's rule, "foreign journalists wishing to conduct news coverage and reporting activities in Tibet Autonomous Region should apply to the FAO of Tibet Autonomous Region for the Approval Letter on Entering Tibet first. Only with the approval letter can they go to Tibet to make interviews and reporting." Retrieved from http://ipc.fmprc.gov.cn/eng/wgjzzhzn/t716854.htm

12 FCCC (2016) Tibet Survey.

13 NPR. (October 3, 2018). Transcript: NPR's Interview With China's Ambassador To The U.S. Retrieved from https://www.npr.org/2018/10/03/654088777/transcript-nprs-interview-with-china-s-ambassador-to-the-u-s?t=1551717634310

14 International Press Center. (November 25, 2015). International Press Center Organizes Tibet Reporting Trip for Foreign Correspondents. Retrieved from http://www.mfa.gov.cn/web/zwbd_673032/ywfc_673029/t1318328.shtml

15 International Press Center. (October 13, 2015). Invitation to a Reporting Trip to Tibet. Retrieved from http://ipc.fmprc.gov.cn/eng/hdtz/t1305401.htm

16 Personal communication, January, 2016.

17 International Press Center. (October 13, 2015). Invitation to a Reporting Trip to Tibet. Retrieved from http://ipc.fmprc.gov.cn/eng/hdtz/t1305401.htm; Martin, P. (January 24, 2019). Inside Xinjiang: a 10-day tour of China's most repressed state. Retrieved from https://www.bloomberg.com/news/features/2019-01-24/inside-the-vast-police-state-at-the-heart-of-china-s-belt-and-road

18 Ramzy, A. & Wong, E. (August 3, 2018). China forces out Buzzfeed journalist. *The New York Times*. Retrieved from https://www.nytimes.com/2018/08/23/world/asia/china-buzzfeed-reporter.html

19 MOFA. (December 26, 2015). (in Chinese) Foreign Ministry Spokesperson Lu Kang's Remarks on the Decision of not Renewing Press Credentials for Ursula Gauthier, a Beijing-based Correspondent for French News Magazine *L'Obs*. Retrieved from https://www.fmprc.gov.cn/mfa_eng/xwfw_665399/s2510_665401/2535_665405/t1328156.shtml

20 Anonymous. (September 25, 2016). (in Chinese) This is what happened when some Western journalists are allowed into Tibet. Retrieved from http://news.ifeng.com/a/20160925/50021477_0.shtml

21 The story on the link between China's richest businessman Wang Jianlin and top political leaders, including Xi, was never run. After Mike Forsythe joined *The New York Times*, the paper ran a story on Wang. See Forsythe, M. (2015, April 28). Wang Jianlin, a billionaire at the intersection of business and power in China. *The New York Times*. Retrieved from www.nytimes.com/2015/04/29/world/asia/wang-jianlin-abillionaire-at-the-intersection-of-business-and-power-in-china.html?_r=0

22 Smith, C. (March 31, 2017). The New York Times vs. the 'Great Firewall' of China. Retrieved from https://www.nytimes.com/2017/03/31/insider/the-new-york-times-vs-the-great-firewall-of-china.html

23 Personal communication, November, 2015.

24 For example, *The Guardian* journalist Tom Phillips has publicly complained on Twitter about pages being ripped out of his copy of *The Economist*: https://twitter.com/tomphillipsin/status/973438929633505280

25 BBC. (October 15, 2014). How Chinese state blocks foreign TV broadcasts. Retrieved from https://www.bbc.co.uk/news/av/world-asia-china-29630910/how-chinese-state-blocks-foreign-tv-broadcasts

26 Personal communication, February, 2016.

27 During an anti-Japan protest in September 2012 in Xi'an, a local man had his skull smashed in for driving a Japanese car.

28 China Daily. (April 2, 2008). CNN: What's wrong with you? Retrieved from http://www.chinadaily.com.cn/china/2008-04/02/content_6587120_2.htm

29 Li, B. (April 7, 2008). CNN biased coverage comes under fire. Retrieved from http://www.cctv.com/english/20080417/106906.shtml

30 See, e.g., Qing, M. (July 27, 2009). (in Chinese). German media badmouthing China with 'Chinese spies' fabrication. *Global Times*. Retrieved from http://world.huanqiu.com/roll/2009-07/527567.html?agt=61

31 Wang, J. (May 7, 2017). Misleading views of intent behind Belt and Road still common in Western media. *Global Times*. Retrieved from http://www.global times.cn/content/1045739.shtml

32 For the script of the Reuters interview, see www.reuters.com/article/us-china-britain-xi-q-a/exclusive-qa-with-chinese-president-xi-jinping-idUSKCN0SC03920151018

33 A full transcript of the interview can be found at www.wsj.com/articles/full-transcript-interview-with-chinese-president-xi-jinping-1442894700?mg=prod/accounts-wsj

34 On a five-point scale, 101 respondents rated harassment at an average score of 2.80 ($SD = 1.11$); access blockage is rated fairly high ($M = 4.16$, $SD = .86$).

35 Personal communication, April, 2016.

36 Personal communication, February, 2016.

37 Personal communication, January, 2016.

38 VanderKlippe, N. (2017, August 25). Detained in 'the safest place' on Earth. *The Globe and Mail*, p. A16.

39 HuffPost. (August 23, 2017). Globe and Mail correspondent Nathan Vander-Klippe briefly detained in China. Retrieved from http://www.huffingtonpost.ca/2017/08/23/globe-and-mail-correspondent-nathan-vanderklippe-briefly-de tained-in-china_a_23159351/:

40 CPJ statement: https://cpj.org/2017/08/chineseauthorities-briefly-detain-globe-and-mail-.php RSF statement: https://rsf.org/en/news/rsf-condemns-harassment-foreign-media-china IFJ statement: https://www.ifj.org/es/centro-de-medios/

noticias/detalle/category/press-releases/article/foreign-journalist-blocked-from-reporting-in-xinjiang.html

41 See video: BBC stopped from visiting China independent candidate. Retrieved from https://www.bbc.co.uk/news/av/world-asia-38005603/bbc-stopped-from-visiting-china-independent-candidate

42 As of January 15, 2017.

43 Personal communication with Al Jazeera English executive producer Owen Watson, March 5, 2015.

44 Jun, Y. (August 30, 2012). German journalists in China ask for Merkel's help. Retrieved from http://www.dw.com/en/german-journalists-in-china-ask-for-merkels-help/a-16207637

45 Personal communication, February, 2016.

46 *The Guardian.* (January 1, 2016). The Guardian view on the foreign press in China: expelling the messenger. Retrieved from https://www.theguardian.com/commentisfree/2016/jan/01/the-guardian-view-on-the-foreign-press-in-china-expelling-the-messenger

7 Conclusion

Reporting the unreportable China?

In the age of globalization amid a changing global order, the field of foreign correspondence in China is of significant relevance to the construction of China as the major rising global power for policy makers and publics around the globe. China correspondents are key agents in the process of reality construction, structured by various power relations. This book mainly taps on the role of the habitus of individual journalists, the journalistic logic in newsrooms and in the press corps as an interpretative community, and state coercion of the host country as well as media cultures in various home countries. It aims to reveal how foreign correspondents respond to pressures from within the journalistic field (such as a transforming media industry), as well as from the changing global geopolitics, and China's increasingly restrictive journalistic culture.

Based on the case of China correspondents in Xi Jinping's 'New Era,' this book explores the conceptualization of a 'field of foreign correspondence' and looks into the structure and dynamics of this field, in relation to the power exerted from the broader field (especially the political field) in a transnational context. The biggest benefit of studying foreign correspondence from a field perspective is that it puts foreign correspondents' news production in a relational set of powers both within and outside the field of foreign correspondence, emphasizing the vital role of 'positioning,' which is both structured and structuring the news production. Hence, this book does not just examine individual journalists or a certain newsroom. Nor does it restrict its focus only to macro-level national systems. Instead, it takes what Bourdieu calls a structuralist-constructivist field perspective to analyze the relationship between agency and structure in foreign correspondence. Journalists as agents have their individual habitus structured during what van Ginneken notes as the three levels of socialization, and the various habitus and capital these agents possess in turn structure their different positions in the field. Journalists are subject to positional pressures coming from both within the field and externally. They do not just passively submit to these pressures, nor do they defy pressures in full swing; they negotiate with them, while actively seeking to secure their position in the field and accumulating more capital. Their various positions structure their different negotiation strategies and affect how they perceive various pressures on their work.

In this final concluding reflecting chapter I firstly pinpoint key findings of this study and put together all key influencers identified at different levels in previous chapters for a comparative glance; then, I reflect on the limitations of this study and the outlook for the nexus between foreign press and China's role in the world.

Habitus and prisms: perceived hierarchical influencers

The changes in political economy and geopolitics in the world bring vital dynamics to the field of China correspondence, firstly by bringing in more competitors, or new entrants, into the field, as a China stint is becoming a reputed position that more journalists are vying for. As Chapter 2 summarized, China correspondence has entered into the 'new era' of reporting a rising and assertive China.

In this 'new era,' China's state coercive pressures on the press are intensifying the power struggles between journalistic autonomy and external powers in the field of China correspondence. Chapter 3 to Chapter 6 are devoted to mapping the pressures from various power relations and journalists' negotiating with these pressures. Chapter 3 analyzed the habitus of China correspondents as operationalized into 'Chinese habitus' and 'journalistic habitus,' and based on their habitus-led positions in the field proposed a typology of four: *Spiralists*, *Sporadics*, *Sinophiles*, and *Sinojournos*. Chapter 4 and Chapter 5 focussed on how journalistic logic within the field plays out on influencing China correspondents' news production. Chapter 4 discussed the organizational control in newsrooms, while Chapter 5 examined the foreign press corps as an interpretative community and their collective reference practice. Chapter 6 focussed on China's uncodified state coercion as major external interruptive forces to control and cramp the practice of foreign press, arguing that both real and imagined pressures of the 'anaconda in the chandelier' lead to China correspondents taking avoidance countermeasures, including self-censorship.

The construction of China news is happening in the field structured by all these forces, including economic and technological factors, which this book intentionally left out. Various factors work together to shape the prisms of China correspondents, which shape the final news discourse on China. It is difficult to say which factor exerts the most pressure on China correspondents and thus plays the primary role in shaping the news discourse. But it might shed some light to compare how journalists themselves perceive the influencing power of the identified factors, altogether in one glance.

Table 7.1 shows a t-test result of China correspondents' perceived influence from various constraints. In general, China correspondents perceive hierarchical levels of influence. Individual habitus, both journalistic ('professional value') and Chinese ('China-related experience'), and difficulty in information access in host China are perceived as the most influential among all identified forces shaping their news production. Individual habitus is important not only in that it directly influences journalists' practice in the field, but also in that habitus lands journalists into different positions, which in turn structure their negotiation strategies. As laid out in Chapter 3, Sinophiles, Sinojournos, Spiralists, and Sporadics act differently in the field, due to their varying habitus (both Chinese and journalistic). For example, Sinophiles and Sporadics may have less interest in challenging or changing the existing power structures in the field of China correspondence.

The difficulty in accessing information in China is perceived as another influential constraint for foreign press, echoing the general assumption of difficulties in reporting in a highly restrictive authoritarian state, where journalists' access to information and sources is strictly controlled. The restrictive laws and regulations in China are also an important constraint, but not as highly rated as information access. As discussed in Chapter 2, codified regulations in the field of China correspondence are strict yet thin: there is not much room for foreign journalists to negotiate with codified

Table 7.1 Perceived Influence from Constraints at Four Levels

Level	Influencer	M	SD	t
Habitus	Personal value	2.89	.98	−1.12
	Professional value	4.16	.91	12.74***
	China-related experience	4.35	.83	16.31***
News organization	Resource	3.22	1.08	2.02*
	Home editor	2.99	1.17	−.09
	Management	2.41	1.16	−5.15***
	Newsroom peers	2.59	1.14	−3.57***
Journalistic community	Competitors	2.88	1.04	−1.15
	Other FCs	2.43	.96	−5.99***
Host country	Press release	2.25	1.05	−7.18***
	Information access	4.16	.86	13.58***
	Chinese law/regulations	3.40	1.20	3.32***
	Chinese government	2.51	1.31	−3.80***
	State coercion	2.80	1.11	−1.79

* $p < .05$
*** $p < .001$

control exerted via credentials regulations, for which every journalist ready to step in the field of China correspondence has been much prepared. Not a law-based society, China coerces foreign press mainly through uncodified means rather than codified laws. These uncodified coercive apparatuses function as what Hassid (2008) calls 'regime of uncertainty,' working more effectively especially in coercing journalists into self-censorship. But as perceived by journalists themselves, harassment, for example, as a pervasive uncodified coercive control is only reported as mildly influential. This is partly because journalists have developed various countermeasures to circumvent or negotiate with harassment and other coercive means, as discussed in Chapter 6, and partly because journalists generally do not tend to acknowledge their practice of self-censoring.

China correspondents perceive competitive pressure and organizational constraints within the journalistic field as mildly influential. Organizational resources and home editors are still major concerns for China correspondents geographically far away from home desks. It suggests that even in today's transnational journalistic practice, facilitated by technology and globalization, news organizations still function as the basic institutional unit of news production, further debunking the myth of foreign correspondents as loners.

The hierarchical importance of influencers as perceived by China correspondents shows individual habitus and institutional constraints are seen as the major influencers on journalists' news production. These are what journalists complain about the most: home editors lacking 'Chineseness,' difficult information access, and harsh state coercion. Overall, they value being equipped with adequate knowledge and understanding of China.

A heteronomous field of China correspondence

Although in a 'new era,' the national landscape of the foreign press corps in China is still largely West-dominated. To disentangle the national variance in transnational reporting, especially to locate the role of national media cultures, I classified the correspondents into four media systems based on the home country of their news organizations: three typical media systems of Western democracies, as proposed by Hallin and Mancini (2004, 2012), and one 'non-Western' media system. National variance stemming from each national journalistic field as embedded in the measurement of media system is detected in the patterns of habitus of individual journalists, newsroom social control, collective reference practice in the tribe of China correspondents, and their strategies of coping with the pressures, especially that from the state coercion exerted from the political field in China.

Journalistic pressures, such as routine press review, resource allocation in the newsroom, and the editor-reporter covenant, are largely dictated by the power relations with heteronomous pressures. Chapter 5, in discussing routine press review practice, has shown that agents under stronger market pressure tend to be more 'pack-minded' and that those with an advantageous position in the power relation often lead the pack, whereas those with a less advantageous position follow the pack.

In addition to the strong shaping force from national media cultures on how China correspondents negotiate with pressures at various levels, China's state coercion on foreign press also suggests that the field of China correspondence is highly heteronomous. As this study finds, both real and imagined pressures of the 'anaconda in the chandelier' are felt by journalists in the field and drive them to take avoidance or fighting-back strategies, which inevitably leave a mark on their news production. Cases such as completely dropping a story under pressure from China happen on a regular basis, adding further evidence that China correspondents do not, or cannot, make editorial decisions purely on journalistic logic.

China correspondents, while operating on a journalistic logic, are considerably influenced by heteronomous pressures typically in the forms of state coercion and national media cultures. We hence observe that, on the spectrum between autonomy and heteronomy, the field of China correspondence is evidently situated towards the heteronomous pole. It is subject to strong external pressures from national journalistic fields of home countries, the political and economic fields in China as the host country, and the power relations between home countries and host country, i.e. national interest.

Reflecting on limitations

As an explorative attempt to understand the configuration and structure of transnational news production in authoritarian China, this book does not aim at a comprehensive scrutiny of the field of China correspondence. Foremost, it does not specifically look into the heteronomous pressures from the economic field (such as those from advertisers and audience), especially the techno-economic factors, in shaping the field of China correspondence. Some transformative forces, such as the adoption of social media among China correspondents, have significantly restructured the boundaries and dynamics of the field of China correspondence. Although the discussion in previous chapters is situated in the change of business models of many news organizations, and Chapter 5 briefly tapped on how technology is intensifying imitation among journalists especially in the restrictive host country of China, it is far from an intensive discussion on how techno-economic pressures shape the highly heteronomous field of China correspondence.

Another limitation of this study is that the empirical evidence this book is drawn on largely came from Anglo-American journalists. This is partly because these journalists are the most available sources, outspoken and willing to connect with Chinese academics, partly because of the still strong hold of Anglo-American journalism in the global media culture. But this skewed sample undeniably limits the representativeness and generalization of the results. The sensitivity of this topic in present-day China is one of the major drawbacks that led to such limitation. Although similar challenges can be anticipated in other authoritarian societies, the assertiveness of present-day China is evidently putting more pressure on journalists to participate on record in such research.

In addition, the relatively narrow definition of 'foreign correspondents' used in this study should be noticed. I chose the official definition of foreign correspondents by PRC China, excluding correspondents from Taiwan, Hong Kong, and Macau, which are either autonomous or semi-autonomous Chinese societies different from PRC China. Coming from similar Chinese cultural background, they are bestowed with advantageous Chinese habitus and are subject to different sets of power relations compared with their foreign counterparts. News produced by journalists from this part of the world provides foreign correspondents important sources of reference. The *South China Morning Post* of Hong Kong, for example, is a closely watched source for news ideas for many English-speaking correspondents working in greater China. In addition, the fact that Hong Kong still serves as the Asian hub for most Western news organizations[1] is also a driving factor for the community of Hong Kong-based journalists, and this community helps shape the news discourse of China. These are all important factors but are not included in the discussion in this book.

Outlook of China correspondence and final note

As China is posing in full momentum to take a leading role in the changing global order and pressing global issues (such as climate change), timely and trusted journalistic accounts and interpretation of this rising power is in high demand in the international community. The field of China correspondence has all impetus to thrive. But its heteronomous nature is worth noting, as external non-journalistic pressures are cramping the autonomous space of China reporting, rendering it unreportable.

How unreportable is authoritarian China, especially in the 'New Era' under Xi Jinping's reign? To begin with, in foreign correspondence the social and cultural gap between the host and home countries poses innate difficulties for any foreign correspondents to sufficiently understand and report a host country, thus independent researching and reporting is almost impossible for many foreign correspondents without the toolkit of language skills and cultural understanding. Such innate 'unreportability' is further pained by a series of China's restrictive regulations, such as forbidding Chinese nationals from working for foreign media. Although Chapter 3 notes that the current generation of China correspondents on average are more China-attuned than their predecessors, the mild change in the configuration of the field is still far from a positive addition to combat the unreportability. This echoes what field theorists hold, that new entrants coming into the field bring demographic or morphological changes to the field, but they are mostly only conformist, thus contributing to reproduction of the field.

Adding to the blow to the field's autonomy is uncodified state coercion. These disruptive external forces are not expected to be alleviated to any degree in the foreseeable future, given the current leadership's governance pattern. But backlashes have already spoken volume. As discussed in previous chapters, lack of access both forces and justifies journalists to pack together, homogenizing story frames and news sources (most probably unfavourable to Chinese government); harassing journalists and their sources prompts journalists, or at least those with positional advantage, to expose and thus to play up the harassment, which only works to embarrass Chinese government in the international community. The negative image of an 'oppressive regime' that has been associated with China since Tiananmen is never to be cast off, should the reminiscence of coercion and oppression remain a reoccurring theme in mainstream international news discourse.

Yet most of the journalists' countermeasures to cope with the external pressure do not in effect challenge the existing power relations. On most occasions, the power struggles during news production are only reproducing the power structure. This is a damning, vicious cycle for both China and the international community. China yearns for a favourable international environment for its global rise and domestic stability. The world needs more diverse media frames with less monotonous China stories, for making each country's own policies at home as well as for cooperating with China in tackling global problems.

It has to be acknowledged that aside from the restrictive journalistic environment in China, heteronomous pressures remain prominent as national interests and national journalistic culture of the home countries of China correspondents will continue to keep a strong grip over news production. One observation is that China correspondents are experiencing rising pressure from their home management, as Chinese diplomats worldwide are becoming increasingly assertive to voice to media management their discontent about news coverage against China's interest.[2] But as one can observe a tendency towards a globalized journalistic culture within the globalization in the broader social space, even though it is only partial and mild, there is reason to believe that given a change to less restrictive coercion on the press and civil society in China, the theme of 'unreportable' fades in reporting China, and both China and the international community benefit.

Notes

1 *The New York Times*, AP, Reuters, *Financial Times*, and CNN all operate their Asian headquarters in Hong Kong.
2 In October 2018, the Chinese Embassy in Germany lodged an official complaint against German newspaper *Sueddeutsche Zeitung* for an interview with the Foreign Minister of Taiwan, which China considers to be part of its territory. See www.chinadaily.com.cn/a/201810/28/WS5bd4f6e5a310eff303284f7b.html

References

Allen-Ebrahimian, B. (2016, March 4). How China won the war against Western media. *Foreign Policy*. Retrieved from http://foreignpolicy.com/2016/03/04/china-won-war-western-media-censorship-propaganda-communist-party/

Anderlini, J. (2014, May 26). China clamps down on US consulting groups. *Financial Times*. Retrieved from www.ft.com/content/310d29ea-e263-11e3-89fd-00144feabdc0

Anonymous. (2016, September 25). *This is what happened when some Western journalists are allowed into Tibet*. Retrieved from http://news.ifeng.com/a/20160925/50021477_0.shtml

Armstrong, C. L. (2004). The influence of reporter gender on source selection in newspaper stories. *Journalism & Mass Communication Quarterly, 81*(1), 139–154.

Bailey, G. A., & Lichty, L. W. (1972). Rough justice on a Saigon street: A gatekeeper study of NBC's Tet execution film. *Journalism Quarterly, 49*(2), 221–238.

Barboza, D. (2012, October 5). Billions in hidden riches for family of Chinese leader. *The New York Times*. Retrieved from www.nytimes.com/2012/10/26/business/global/family-of-wen-jiabao-holds-a-hidden-fortune-in-china.html

Barma, N. H., & Ratner, E. (2006). China's illiberal challenge. *Democracy: A Journal of Ideas*, (2) (Fall), 56–68.

BBC. (2014, October 15). *How Chinese state blocks foreign TV broadcasts*. Retrieved from www.bbc.co.uk/news/av/world-asia-china-29630910/how-chinese-state-blocks-foreign-tv-broadcasts

BBC. (2017, August 17). *Chinese media "racist" video on India clash sparks anger*. Retrieved from www.bbc.com/news/world-asia-china-40957719

Becker, L., Lowrey, W., Claussen, D., & Anderson, W. (2000). Why does the beat go on? *Newspaper Research Journal, 21*(4), 2–16.

Beckett, C., & Mansell, R. (2008). Crossing boundaries: New media and networked journalism. *Communication, Culture & Critique, 1*(1), 92–104.

Bennett, A. (1990). American reporters in China: Romantics and cynics. In *Voices of China: The interplay of politics and journalism* (pp. 263–276). New York, NY: Guilford Press.

Benson, R. (1999). Field theory in comparative context: A new paradigm for media studies. *Theory and Society, 28*(3), 463–498.

Benson, R. (2005). Mapping field variation: Journalism in France and the United States. In *Bourdieu and the journalistic field* (pp. 85–112). Malden, MA: Polity Press.

Benson, R. (2006). News media as a "journalistic field": What Bourdieu adds to new institutionalism, and vice versa. *Political Communication, 23*(2), 187–202.

Benson, R., & Hallin, D. C. (2007). How states, markets and globalization shape the news: The French and US national press, 1965–97. *European Journal of Communication, 22*(1), 27–48.

Boczkowski, P. J. (2010). *News at work: Imitation in an age of information abundance.* Chicago: University of Chicago Press.

Bourdieu, P. (1977). *Outline of a theory of practice.* Cambridge: Cambridge University Press.

Bourdieu, P. (1983). The field of cultural production, or: The economic world reversed. *Poetics, 12*(4–5), 311–356.

Bourdieu, P. (1985). The genesis of the concepts of habitus and field. *Sociocriticism, 2*(2), 11–24.

Bourdieu, P. (1986). The forms of capital. In *Handbook of theory and research for the sociology of education* (pp. 241–258). New York, NY: Greenwood Press.

Bourdieu, P. (1989). Social space and symbolic power. *Sociological Theory, 7*(1), 14–25.

Bourdieu, P. (1993). *The field of cultural production: Essays on art and literature.* New York, NY: Columbia University Press.

Bourdieu, P. (1994). Theory of symbolic power. *Culture/Power/History: A Reader in Contemporary Social Theory, 155.*

Bourdieu, P. (1996). *The rules of art: Genesis and structure of the literary field.* Stanford, CA: Stanford University Press.

Bourdieu, P. (1998). *On television* (P. P. Ferguson, Trans.). New York, NY: New Press.

Bourdieu, P. (2005). The political field, the social science field, and the journalistic field. In *Bourdieu and the journalistic field* (pp. 29–47). Malden, MA: Polity Press.

Bourdieu, P., & Wacquant, L. J. D. (1992). *An invitation to reflexive sociology.* Chicago: University of Chicago Press.

Breed, W. (1955). Social control in the newsroom: A functional analysis. *Social Forces,* 326–335.

Brownlie, S. (2014). Examining self-censorship. In *Modes of censorship: National contexts and diverse media* (pp. 213–242). Abingdon, UK: Routledge.

Brüggemann, Michael, Edda Humprecht, Rasmus Kleis Nielsen, Kari Karppinen, Alessio Cornia, and Frank Esser. (2016). Framing the newspaper crisis: How debates on the state of the press are shaped in Finland, France, Germany, Italy, United Kingdom and United States. *Journalism Studies, 17*(5), 533–551.

Byerly, C. M., & Ross, K. (2006). *Women and media: A critical introduction.* Hoboken, NJ: John Wiley & Sons.

Campbell, K., & Ratner, E. (2018). The China reckoning. *Foreign Affairs.* Retrieved from www.foreignaffairs.com/articles/china/2018-02-13/china-reckoning

Carey, James W. (2001). Lawyers, voyeurs and vigilantes. In *What's next? The problems and prospects of journalism* (pp. 19–25). New Brunswick, NJ: Transaction Publishers.

Carlson, M. (2009). Dueling, dancing, or dominating? Journalists and their sources. *Sociology Compass*, *3*(4), 526–542.

Chalaby, J. K. (1996). Journalism as an Anglo-American invention: A comparison of the development of French and Anglo-American journalism, 1830s–1920s. *European Journal of Communication*, *11*(3), 303–326.

Chalaby, J. K. (1998). *The invention of journalism*. Basingstoke, Hampshire; New York, NY: Palgrave Macmillan.

Chalaby, J. K. (2000). New media, new freedoms, new threats. *Gazette (Leiden, Netherlands)*, *62*(1), 19–29.

Champagne, P. (1999). The view from the media. In P. Bourdieu, et al., *The weight of the world: Social suffering in contemporary society* (pp. 45–59). Cambridge: Polity Press.

Chan, J. M., & Lee, C.-C. (1988). Press ideology and organizational control in Hong Kong. *Communication Research*, *15*(2), 185–197.

Chan, M. K. (2017). Reporting from China: 400 reports, on 1.4 billion people, in One authoritarian state. *International Journal of Communication*, *11*.

Chen, J., & Wang, Y. (2009). Foreign media in China (wai mei zou zhongguo). *China News Weekly*. Retrieved from http://news.sina.com.cn/c/sd/2009-09-23/121518710128_3.shtml

Chin, J. (2016, February 21). China issues broad new rules for web. *Wall Street Journal*. Retrieved from www.wsj.com/articles/china-issues-broad-new-rules-for-web-1455900422

Chin, J. (2017, January 10). How to ride an escalator: China says you're doing it wrong. *The Wall Street Journal*. Retrieved from www.wsj.com/articles/rising-risk-china-reconsiders-stand-right-walk-left-on-escalators-1484029173

China Daily. (2008, April 2). CNN: What's wrong with you? Retrieved from www.chinadaily.com.cn/china/2008-04/02/content_6587120_2.htm

Chong, S. (2018, July 4). (in Chinese). Smearing China, Western media slap themselves. *Cankao Xiaoxi*. Retrieved from http://column.cankaoxiaoxi.com/2018/0704/2287945.shtml

Chu, J. (1984). The gathering of news about China. *Gazette (Leiden, Netherlands)*, *33*(2), 87–106.

Clayman, S. E., & Reisner, A. (1998). Gatekeeping in action: Editorial conferences and assessments of newsworthiness. *American Sociological Review*, 178–199.

Cohen, B. C. (1963). *Press and foreign policy*. Princeton, NJ: Princeton University Press.

Cook, S. (2016, January 6). Chinese journalism, interrupted. *Foreign Policy*. Retrieved from https://foreignpolicy.com/2016/01/06/chinese-journalism-interrupted-what-government-censored-in-2015/

Corcoran, F., & Fahy, D. (2009). Exploring the European elite sphere: The role of the Financial Times. *Journalism Studies*, *10*(1), 100–113.

Coronel, S. (2012). The Bo scandal: How we got that story. *Columbia Journalism Review*. Retrieved from http://archives.cjr.org/behind_the_news/the_bo_scandal_how_we_got_that.php

Couldry, N. (2003). Media and symbolic power: Extending the range of Bourdieu's field theory. *Media@ lse Electronic Working Papers Department of Media and Communications, LSE, 2*.

Craft, S., & Wanta, W. (2004). Women in the newsroom: Influences of female editors and reporters on the news agenda. *Journalism & Mass Communication Quarterly, 81*(1), 124–138.

Cross, A. (2018). "Stop overlooking us!": Missed intersections of Trump, media, and rural America. In *The Trump presidency, journalism, and democracy* (pp. 231–256). Abingdon, UK: Routledge.

Crouse, T. (1973). *The boys on the bus: Riding with the campaign press corps*. New York, NY: Random House.

Darras, E. (2005). Media consecration of the political order. In V. R. Benson & E. Neveu (Eds.), *Bourdieu and the journalistic field* (pp. 156–173). Malden, MA: Polity Press.

de Burgh, H. (2004). *The Chinese journalist: Mediating information in the world's most populous country*. Abingdon, UK: Routledge.

de Grandpre, A. (2017, August 17). Chinese state media made a racist video about India and is censoring its critics. *The Washington Post*. Retrieved from www.washingtonpost.com/news/worldviews/wp/2017/08/17/chinese-state-media-made-a-racist-video-about-india-and-is-censoring-its-critics/?utm_term=.9de417253240

Denyer, S. (2017, April 14). Chocolate cake and chemistry repair U.S.-China ties: But will North Korea spoil the party? *The Washington Post*. Retrieved from www.washingtonpost.com/world/chocolate-cake-and-chemistry-repair-us-china-ties-but-will-north-korea-spoil-the-party/2017/04/14/5cf5a950-206e-11e7-bb59-a74ccaf1d02f_story.html?

Deuze, M. (2005). What is journalism? Professional identity and ideology of journalists reconsidered. *Journalism, 6*(4), 442–464.

Dickinson, R. (2008). Studying the sociology of journalists: The journalistic field and the news world. *Sociology Compass, 2*(5), 1383–1399.

Dobson, W. (2018, October 2). *China unbound: What an emboldened China means for the world*. Retrieved from www.npr.org/2018/10/02/653312942/china-unbound-what-an-emboldened-china-means-for-the-world

Donsbach, W. (2009). Journalists and their professional identities. In *The Routledge companion to news and journalism* (pp. 82–92). Abingdon, UK: Routledge.

Donsbach, W., & Patterson, T. E. (2004). Political news journalists. *Comparing Political Communication: Theories, Cases, and Challenges*, 251–270.

Dunaway, J. (2008). Markets, ownership, and the quality of campaign news coverage. *The Journal of Politics, 70*(4), 1193–1202.

Earp, M. (2012, May 8). *China ducks questions about Al-Jazeera expulsion*. Committee to Protect Journalists. Retrieved from https://cpj.org/blog/2012/05/china-ducks-questions-about-al-jazeera-expulsion.php

Ebo, B. (1997). Media diplomacy and foreign policy: Toward a theoretical framework. *News Media and Foreign Relations: A Multifaceted Perspective*, 43–57.

Ember, S. (2016, September 17). New York Times reinstates managing editor role and appoints Joseph Kahn. *The New York Times*, p. B5.

Emery, M. (1989). An endangered species: The international newshole. *Gannett Center Journal, 3*(4), 151–164.

Esser, F. (1998). Editorial structures and work principles in British and German newsrooms. *European Journal of Communication, 13*(3), 375–405.

Esser, F. (2008). Dimensions of political news cultures: Sound bite and image bite news in France, Germany, Great Britain, and the United States. *The International Journal of Press/Politics*, *13*(4), 401–428.

Farmer, E. L. (1990). Sifting truth from facts: The reporter as interpreter of China. *Voices of China: The Interplay of Politics and Journalism*, 243–262.

Feng, E., & Kazmin, A. (2017, August 17). Chinese video mocks India over Himalayas border stand-off. *Financial Times*. Retrieved from www.ft.com/content/0dbfbb60-8300-11e7-a4ce-15b2513cb3ff

Fishman, M. (1988). *Manufacturing the news*. Austin: University of Texas Press.

Fleeson, L. (2003). Bureau of missing bureaus. *American Journalism Review*, *25*(7), 32–40.

Foreign Correspondents Club of China. (2016). *Conditions for Foreign Media in China 2015 report*. Retrieved from https://china.usc.edu/foreign-correspondents-club-china-conditions-foreign-media-china-april-4-2016

Foreign Correspondents Club of China. (2018). *Access denied: FCCC 2017 report*. Retrieved from https://www.dropbox.com/s/95ghn59rl93ceu9/Access%20Denied-FCCC%20report%202017.pdf?dl=0

Foreign Correspondents Club of China. (2019). *Under watch: FCCC 2018 report*. Retrieved from https://www.dropbox.com/s/h2h00yicr2eusyt/under%20watch.pdf?dl=0

French, H. (2014). Bloomberg's folly. *Columbia Journalism Review*. Retrieved from http://archives.cjr.org/feature/bloombergs_folly.php

French, P. (2009). *Through the looking glass: China's foreign journalists from opium wars to Mao* (Vol. 1). Hong Kong: Hong Kong University Press.

Fu, N. C. (1990). Reporting on China from Washington: Some observations and reflections. In C. C. Lee (Ed.), *Voices of China: The interplay of politics and journalism* (pp. 288–95). New York, NY: Guilford Press.

Gade, P. J. (2008). Journalism guardians in a time of great change: Newspaper editors' perceived influence in integrated news organizations. *Journalism & Mass Communication Quarterly*, *85*(2), 371–392.

Gallagher, M. (2008). At the millennium: Shifting patterns in gender, culture and journalism. *Women Journalists in the Western World*, s., 201–216.

Gans, H. J. (1979). *Deciding what's news: A study of CBS evening news, NBC nightly news, newsweek, and time*. New York, NY: Random House.

Gans, H. J. (2003). *Democracy and the news*. Oxford: Oxford University Press.

Gerschewski, J. (2013). The three pillars of stability: Legitimation, repression, and co-optation in autocratic regimes. *Democratization*, *20*(1), 13–38.

Gitlin, T. (2003). *The whole world is watching: Mass media in the making and unmaking of the new left*. Berkeley: University of California Press.

Golan, G. (2006). Inter-media agenda setting and global news coverage: Assessing the influence of the New York Times on three network television evening news programs. *Journalism Studies*, *7*(2), 323–333.

Goldkorn, J. (2017, March 16). *Chris Buckley: The China journalist's China journalist*. Retrieved from https://supchina.com/podcast/chris-buckley-china-journalists-china-journalist/

Grigg, A. (2016, September 24). China's new invasion of Tibet. *Australian Financial Review*. Retrieved from www.afr.com/lifestyle/chinas-new-invasion-of-tibet-20160919-grjjsy

Grigg, A., & Murray, L. (2016, March 24). The cult of Xi Jinping. *Australian Financial Review*, 24.

The Guardian. (2016, January 1). The Guardian view on the foreign press in China: Expelling the messenger. Retrieved from www.theguardian.com/commentisfree/2016/jan/01/the-guardian-view-on-the-foreign-press-in-china-expelling-the-messenger

Hachten, W. A., & Scotton, J. F. (2011). *The world news prism: Challenges of digital communication*. Hoboken, NJ: John Wiley & Sons.

Hahn, O., & Lönnendonker, J. (2009). Transatlantic foreign reporting and foreign correspondents after 9/11: Trends in reporting Europe in the United States. *The International Journal of Press/Politics*, *14*(4), 497–515.

Hallin, D. C. (1992). The passing of the "high modernism" of American journalism. *Journal of Communication*, *42*(3), 14–25.

Hallin, D. C. (2005). Field theory, differentiation theory, and comparative media research. *Bourdieu and the Journalistic Field*, 224–243.

Hallin, D. C., & Mancini, P. (2004). *Comparing media systems: Three models of media and politics*. Cambridge: Cambridge University Press.

Hamilton, J. M., & Jenner, E. (2004). Redefining foreign correspondence. *Journalism*, *5*(3), 301–321.

Handley, R. L., & Rutigliano, L. (2012). Journalistic field wars: Defending and attacking the national narrative in a diversifying journalistic field. *Media, Culture & Society*, *34*(6), 744–760.

Hanitzsch, T. (2007). Deconstructing journalism culture: Toward a universal theory. *Communication Theory*, *17*(4), 367–385.

Hanitzsch, T., et al. (2010). Modeling perceived influences on journalism: Evidence from a cross-national survey of journalists. *Journalism & Mass Communication Quarterly*, *87*(1), 5–22.

Hanitzsch, T., et al. (2011). Mapping journalism cultures across nations: A comparative study of 18 countries. *Journalism Studies*, *12*(3), 273–293.

Hanitzsch, T., & Hanusch, F. (2012). Does gender determine journalists' professional views? A reassessment based on cross-national evidence. *European Journal of Communication*, *27*(3), 257–277.

Hannerz, U. (2004). *Foreign news: Exploring the world of foreign correspondents*. Chicago: University of Chicago Press.

Hannerz, U. (2007). Foreign correspondents and the varieties of cosmopolitanism. *Journal of Ethnic and Migration Studies*, *33*(2), 299–311.

Harding, H. (1990). Journalists, scholars, officials: The case of Sino-American relations. In *Voices of China: The interplay of politics and journalism*. New York, NY: Guilford Press.

Hargreaves, I. (2003). *Journalism: Truth or dare?* Oxford: Oxford University Press.

Hassid, J. (2008). Controlling the Chinese media: An uncertain business. *Asian Survey*, *48*(3), 414–430.

Hassid, J. (2011). Four models of the fourth estate: A typology of contemporary Chinese journalists. *The China Quarterly, 208*, 813–832.

Hedman, U. (2015). J-Tweeters: Pointing towards a new set of professional practices and norms in journalism. *Digital Journalism, 3*(2), 279–297.

Herman, E. S., & Chomsky, N. (1988). *Manufacturing consent: The political economy of the mass media.* New York: Pantheon Books.

Hermida, A. (2010). Twittering the news: The emergence of ambient journalism. *Journalism Practice, 4*(3), 297–308.

Hernández, J. (2017, August 17). Chinese video on border standoff with India provokes accusations of racism. *The New York Times.* Retrieved from www. nytimes.com/2017/08/17/world/asia/china-india-racist-video-border-standoff. html?_r=0

Hesmondhalgh, D. (2006). Bourdieu, the media and cultural production. *Media, Culture & Society, 28*(2), 211–231.

Hess, S. (1996). *International news and foreign correspondents* (Vol. 5). Washington, DC: Brookings Institution Press.

Hess, S. (2005). *Through their eyes: Foreign correspondents in the United States* (Vol. 6). Washington, D.C.: Brookings Institution Press.

Hewitt, D. (2001, February 18). Shanghai: Old meets new. *BBC News.* Retrieved from http://news.bbc.co.uk/2/hi/programmes/from_our_own_correspondent/117 4104.stm

Hohenberg, J. (1967). *Between two worlds: Policy, press, and public opinion in Asian-American relations.* New York: FA Praeger.

Hovden, J. F. (2008). *Profane and sacred: A study of the Norwegian journalistic field* (Doctoral Dissertation). Norway: The University of Bergen.

Høyer, S. (2005). The idea of the book: Introduction. In *Diffusion of the news paradigm 1850–2000* (pp. 9–16). Göteborg: Nordicom.

HuffPost. (2017, August 23). Globe and Mail correspondent Nathan VanderKlippe briefly detained in China. Retrieved from www.huffingtonpost.ca/2017/08/23/ globe-and-mail-correspondent-nathan-vanderklippe-briefly-detained-in-china_ a_23159351/

Hummel, R., Kirchhoff, S., & Prandner, D. (2012). "We used to be queens and now we are slaves" working conditions and career strategies in the journalistic field. *Journalism Practice, 6*(5–6), 722–731.

International Press Center. (2015, October 13). *Invitation to a reporting trip to Tibet.* Retrieved from http://ipc.fmprc.gov.cn/eng/hdtz/t1305401.htm

International Press Center. (2015, November 25). International press center organizes Tibet. *Reporting Trip for Foreign Correspondents.* Retrieved from www. mfa.gov.cn/web/zwbd_673032/ywfc_673029/t1318328.shtml

Jarvis, J. (2006). Networked journalism. *Buzz Machine, 5.*

Johnson, I. (2018). *China watching: Language wars, from Montreal to Beijing.* Retrieved from http://chinaheritage.net/journal/china-watching-language-wars-from-montreal-to-beijing/

Jun, Y. (2012, August 30). *German journalists in China ask for Merkel's help.* Retrieved from www.dw.com/en/german-journalists-in-china-ask-for-merkels-help/a-16207637

Kaufman, A. A. (2010). The "century of humiliation," then and now: Chinese perceptions of the international order. *Pacific Focus, 25*(1), 1–33.

Kellam, M., & Stein, E. A. (2016). Silencing critics: Why and how presidents restrict media freedom in democracies. *Comparative Political Studies, 49*(1), 36–77.

Kim, K. (2003). Organizational determinants of international news coverage in Korean newspapers. *Gazette (Leiden, Netherlands), 65*(1), 65–85.

King, G., Pan, J., & Roberts, M. E. (2013). How censorship in China allows government criticism but silences collective expression. *American Political Science Review, 107*(2), 326–343.

Kopper, G. G., & Bates, B. J. (2011). The political economy of foreign correspondence. In *Understanding foreign correspondence: A Euro-American handbook of concepts, methodologies, and theories* (pp. 45–68). New York, NY: Peter Lang.

Kristof, N. (2009, June 3). Bullets over Beijing. *The New York Times*. Retrieved from www.nytimes.com/2009/06/04/opinion/04kristof.html?_r=1

Kuhn, R. (1995). *Media in France*. London and New York, NY: Routledge.

Landler, M. (2018, October 3). Pence speech to string together a narrative of Chinese aggression. *The New York Times*. Retrieved from www.nytimes.com/2018/10/03/us/politics/china-pence-trade-military-elections.html

Lang, G. E., & Lang, K. (1955). The inferential structure of political communications: A study in unwitting bias. *Public Opinion Quarterly, 19*(2), 168–183.

Langfitt, F. (2017, January 25). For journalists who've worked in China, new White House tactics seem familiar. *NPR*. Retrieved from www.npr.org/sections/parallels/2017/01/25/511460917/for-journalists-whove-worked-in-china-new-white-house-tactics-seem-familiar

Lee, C.-C. (1990). Mass media: Of China, about China. In *Voices of China: The interplay of politics and journalism* (pp. 3–29). New York, NY: Guilford Press.

Lee, C.-C. (1998). Press self-censorship and political transition in Hong Kong. *Harvard International Journal of Press/Politics, 3*(2), 55–73.

Lee, C.-C. (2000). Chinese communication. *Power, Money, and Media: Communication Patterns and Bureaucratic Control in Cultural China*, 3–44.

Lee, C.-C. (2001). Rethinking political economy: Implications for media and democracy in greater China. *Javnost-the Public, 8*(4), 81–102.

Lee, C.-C. (2002). Established pluralism: US elite media discourse about China policy. *Journalism Studies, 3*(3), 343–357.

Lee, C.-C. (2006). The conception of Chinese journalists: Ideological convergence and contestation. In *Making journalists* (pp. 123–142). Abingdon, UK: Routledge.

Lee, C.-C. (2010). Bound to rise: Chinese media discourses on the new global order. *Reorienting Global Communication: Indian and Chinese Media Beyond Borders*, 260–283.

Lee, C.-C., Li, H., & Lee, F. L. F. (2011). Symbolic use of decisive events: Tiananmen as a news icon in the editorials of the elite US press. *The International Journal of Press/Politics, 16*(3), 335–356.

Lee, F. L. F., & Chan, J. M. (2016). Collective memory mobilization and Tiananmen commemoration in Hong Kong. *Media, Culture & Society, 38*(1), 997–1014.

Lee, P. S. N. (2016). The rise of China and its contest for discursive power. *Global Media and China, 1*(1–2), 102–120.

Lesly, E. (1991). Realtors and builders demand happy news . . . and often get it. *Washington Journalism Review*, *13*(9), 20–23.

Lewis, C. (2018, May 31). Meet the man at the heart of the latest Chinese influence scandal. *Crikey*. Retrieved from www.crikey.com.au/2018/05/31/john-garnaut-just-who-is-the-man-at-the-centre-of-the-latest-china-controversy/

Lewis, S. C. (2012). The tension between professional control and open participation: Journalism and its boundaries. *Information, Communication & Society*, *15*(6), 836–866.

Li, B. (2008, April 7). *CNN biased coverage comes under fire*. Retrieved from www.cctv.com/english/20080417/106906.shtml

Li, H., & Lee, C.-C. (2013). Remembering Tiananmen and the Berlin Wall: The elite US press's anniversary journalism, 1990–2009. *Media, Culture & Society*, *35*(7), 830–846.

Li, P., & Shepherd, C. (2018, March 21). China tightens grip on media with regulator reshuffle. *Reuters*. Retrieved from https://uk.reuters.com/article/uk-china-parliament-media/china-tightens-grip-on-media-with-regulator-reshuffle-idUKKBN1GX0JK

Li, P. S. (2005). The rise and fall of Chinese immigration to Canada: Newcomers from Hong Kong special administrative region of China and Mainland China, 1980–2000. *International Migration*, *43*(3), 9–34.

Li, X. (2016, June 29). Party-backed song raps about foreign media prejudice. *Sixth Tone*. Retrieved from www.sixthtone.com/news/1018/party-backed-group-raps-about-foreign-media-prejudice

Liang, J. (2002). *How U.S. correspondents discover, uncover, and cover China: China-watching transformed* (Vol. 27). Lewiston, NY: Edwin Mellen Press.

Lindell, J. (2015). Bourdieusian media studies: Returning social theory to old and new media. *Distinktion: Scandinavian Journal of Social Theory*, *16*(3), 362–377.

Link, P. (2002). China: The anaconda in the chandelier (Censorship, intellectuals). *New York Review of Books*, *49*(6), 67–70.

Liu, J. (2006, December 1). (in Chinese). *Ministry of foreign affairs press conference*. Retrieved from www.gov.cn/gzdt/2006-12/01/content_459087.htm

Lubman, S. (2015, June 16). China asserts more control over foreign and domestic NGOs. *The Wall Street Journal*. Retrieved from https://blogs.wsj.com/chinarealtime/2015/06/16/china-asserts-more-control-over-foreign-and-domestic-ngos/

MacBride, S. (1980). *Many voices, one world: Towards a new, more just, and more efficient world information and communication order*. London: Kogan Page.

MacLeod, C. (2017, June 20). China's pursuit of artificial intelligence worries America. *The Times*. Retrieved from www.thetimes.co.uk/article/china-s-pursuit-of-artificial-intelligence-worries-america-lhrbhvk5r

Mann, J. (2001). Framing China: A complex country cannot be explained with simplistic formulas. In *Covering China*. New Brunswick, NJ: Transaction Publishers.

Markopoulos, P., De Ruyter, B., & Mackay, W. (2009). *Awareness systems: Advances in theory, methodology and design*. Dordrecht: Springer.

Martin, P. (2019, January 24). *Inside Xinjiang: A 10-day tour of China's most repressed state*. Retrieved from www.bloomberg.com/news/features/2019-01-24/inside-the-vast-police-state-at-the-heart-of-china-s-belt-and-road

Matusitz, J., & Breen, G.-M. (2012). An examination of pack journalism as a form of groupthink: A theoretical and qualitative analysis. *Journal of Human Behavior in the Social Environment, 22*(7), 896–915.

McCluskey, M. (2008). Reporter beat and content differences in environmental stories. *Journalism & Mass Communication Quarterly, 85*(1), 83–98.

McKenzie, N., & O'Malley, N. (2018, May 28). Bob Carr enlists Labor in new China influence row. *The Sydney Morning Herald.* Retrieved from www.smh.com.au/politics/federal/bob-carr-enlists-labor-in-new-china-influence-row-20180528-p4zi0z.html

Merle, P. F. (2013). City of lights? The waning elitism of US correspondents in Paris between 1998 and 2010. *International Communication Gazette, 75*(2), 157–173.

Mills, C. W. (1963). Two styles of social science research. In *Power, politics and people: The collected essays of C. Wright Mills.* New York, NY: Oxford University Press.

Mirsky, J. (2000). Getting the story in China: American reporters since 1972. *Joan Shorenstein Center on the Press, Politics, and Public Policy, Working Paper Series.*

MOFA. (2015, December 26). *Foreign ministry spokesperson Lu Kang's remarks on the decision of not renewing press credentials for Ursula Gauthier, a Beijing-based correspondent for French news magazine L'Obs.* Retrieved from www.fmprc.gov.cn/mfa_eng/xwfw_665399/s2510_665401/2535_665405/t1328156.shtml

Molotch, H., & Lester, M. (1974). News as purposive behavior: On the strategic use of routine events, accidents, and scandals. *American Sociological Review,* 101–112.

Morrison, D. E., & Tumber, H. (1985). The foreign correspondent: Date-line London. *Media, Culture & Society, 7*(4), 445–470.

Mourão, R. R. (2015). The boys on the timeline: Political journalists' use of Twitter for building interpretive communities. *Journalism, 16*(8), 1107–1123.

Murrell, C. (2014). *Foreign correspondents and international newsgathering: The role of fixers.* Abingdon, UK: Routledge.

Nakamura, D., & Wan, W. (2013, December 5). Biden forcefully complains to Chinese leaders about crackdown on foreign news media. *The Washington Post.* Retrieved from www.washingtonpost.com/world/biden-meets-with-journalists-concerned-about-chinas-recent-crackdown-on-foreign-media/2013/12/05/fd3d280e-5d8d-11e3-95c2-13623eb2b0e1_story.html?utm_term=.b8e8aa8108cb

Neveu, E. (2007). Pierre Bourdieu: Sociologist of media, or sociologist for media scholars? *Journalism Studies, 8*(2), 335–347.

NPR. (2018, October 3). Transcript: NPR's interview with China's ambassador to the U.S. Retrieved from www.npr.org/2018/10/03/654088777/transcript-nprs-interview-with-china-s-ambassador-to-the-u-s?t=1551717634310

Oksenberg, M. (1994). The American correspondent in China. In *China's media, media's China* (pp. 205–224). Boulder, CO: Westview Press.

Osnos, E. (2013, July 5). A billion stories. *The New Yorker.* Retrieved from www.newyorker.com/news/evan-osnos/a-billion-stories

Page, J., Spegele, B., & Eder, S. (2012, April 7). "Jackie Kennedy of China" at center of political drama. *The Wall Street Journal.* Retrieved from www.wsj.com/articles/SB10001424052702303299604577327472813686432

Patterson, T. E., & Donsbagh, W. (1996). News decisions: Journalists as partisan actors. *Political Communication, 13*(4), 455–468.

Pearce, K. E. (2015). Democratizing kompromat: The affordances of social media for state-sponsored harassment. *Information, Communication & Society, 18*(10), 1158–1174.

Pedelty, M. (2013). *War stories: The culture of foreign correspondents*. Abingdon, UK: Routledge.

PEN America. (2016). *Darkened screen: Constraints on foreign journalists in China*. Retrieved from https://pen.org/darkened-screen-constraints-on-foreign-journalists-in-china/

Peng, Z. (2004). Representation of China: An across time analysis of coverage in the New York Times and Los Angeles Times. *Asian Journal of Communication, 14*(1), 53–67.

Perlez, J. (2018, February 27). Xi Jinping extends power, and China braces for a new cold war. *The New York Times*. Retrieved from www.nytimes.com/2018/02/27/world/asia/xi-jinping-china-new-cold-war.html

Perlroth, N. (2013, February 2). Washington Post joins list of news media hacked by the Chinese. *The New York Times*, p. B6.

Pew Research Center. (2016, October 5). Chinese public sees more powerful role in world, names U.S. as top threat. Retrieved from www.pewglobal.org/2016/10/05/chinese-public-sees-more-powerful-role-in-world-names-u-s-as-top-threat/

Qian, G., & Bandurski, D. (2011). China's emerging public sphere: The impact of media commercialization, professionalism, and the Internet in an era of transition. *Changing Media, Changing China*, 38–76.

Qian, J. (2012). *Professional community in mobility: A research on foreign correspondents in China* (Doctoral Dissertation). China: Fudan University.

Qian, J. (2015). Analysis on the social interactions among foreign correspondents in China: A transnational social space perspective. *Chinese Journal of Journalism & Communication, 37*(4), 55–70.

Qing, M. (2009, July 27). (in Chinese). German media badmouthing China with "Chinese spies" fabrication. *Global Times*. Retrieved from http://world.huanqiu.com/roll/2009-07/527567.html?agt=61

Qu, X., Su, X., & Li, J. (2012, May 23). (in Chinese). *Western media work with their governments to smear China*. Retrieved from http://world.people.com.cn/GB/17958583.html

Ramzy, A., & Wong, E. (2018, August 3). China forces out Buzzfeed journalist. *The New York Times*. Retrieved from www.nytimes.com/2018/08/23/world/asia/china-buzzfeed-reporter.html

Reese, S. D. (1990). The news paradigm and the ideology of objectivity: A socialist at the Wall Street Journal. *Critical Studies in Media Communication, 7*(4), 390–409.

Reese, S. D., & Danielian, L. H. (1989). Intermedia influence and the drug issue. *Communication Campaigns about Drugs: Government, Media, and the Public*, 29–46.

Reuters. (2017, April 10). *Beijing offers cash rewards to unearth foreign spies*. Retrieved from www.reuters.com/article/us-china-security/beijing-offers-cash-rewards-to-unearth-foreign-spies-idUSKBN17C09S

Revers, M. (2017). Competitive collegiality: The press corps environment. In *Contemporary journalism in the US and Germany* (pp. 113–152). New York, NY: Palgrave Macmillan.

Rosenblum, M. (1979). *Coups and earthquakes: Reporting the world for America*. New York, NY: Joanna Cotler.

Roush, C. (2013, November 13). *Pulitzer winner Bennett leaving Bloomberg*. Retrieved from https://talkingbiznews.com/1/pulitzer-winner-bennett-leaving-bloomberg/

Sambrook, R. (2010). *Are foreign correspondents redundant?* Oxford: Reuters Institute for the Study of Journalism, University of Oxford.

Schudson, M. (2001). The objectivity norm in American journalism. *Journalism, 2*(2), 149–170.

Schudson, M. (2005). Autonomy from what. *Bourdieu and the Journalistic Field, 214*, 214–223.

Schudson, M., & Anderson, C. (2009). Objectivity, professionalism, and truth seeking in journalism. In *The handbook of journalism studies* (pp. 108–121). Abingdon, UK: Routledge.

Schultz, I. (2007). The journalistic gut feeling: Journalistic doxa, news habitus and orthodox news values. *Journalism Practice, 1*(2), 190–207.

Scott, D. K., Gobetz, R. H., & Chanslor, M. (2008). Chain versus independent television station ownership: Toward an investment model of commitment to local news quality. *Communication Studies, 59*(1), 84–98.

Shambaugh, D. (2016). *China's future*. Hoboken, NJ: John Wiley & Sons.

Shear, M. (2014, January 31). White house urges China to act on journalists' visas. *The New York Times*, p. A9.

Shirk, S. L. (Ed.). (2011). *Changing media, changing China*. Oxford: Oxford University Press.

Shoemaker, P. J., & Reese, S. D. (1996). *Mediating the message: Theories of Influences on Mass Media Content*. New York, NY: Longman.

Shoemaker, P. J., & Reese, S. D. (2013). *Mediating the message in the 21st century*. New York, NY and Abingdon, UK: Routledge.

Sigal, L. V. (1973). *Reporters and officials: The organization and politics of newsmaking*. Lexington, MA: Lexington Books.

Sigelman, L. (1973). Reporting the news: An organizational analysis. *American Journal of Sociology, 79*(1), 132–151.

Smith, C. (2017, March 31). *The New York Times vs. the "Great Firewall" of China*. Retrieved from www.nytimes.com/2017/03/31/insider/the-new-york-times-vs-the-great-firewall-of-china.html

Soloski, J. (1989). News reporting and professionalism: Some constraints on the reporting of the news. *Media, Culture & Society, 11*(2), 207–228.

Song, Y., & Lee, C.-C. (2014). Embedded journalism: Constructing romanticized images of China by US journalists in the 1970s. *Chinese Journal of Communication, 7*(2), 174–190.

Song, Y., & Lee, C.-C. (2015). The strategic ritual of irony: Post-Tiananmen China as seen through the "Personalized Journalism" of elite US correspondents. *Media, Culture & Society, 37*(8), 1176–1192.

Song, Y., & Lee, C.-C. (2016). Perceiving different chinas: Paradigm change in the "Personalized Journalism" of elite US journalists, 1976–1989. *International Journal of Communication, 10*, 20.

Starck, K., & Villanueva, E. (1992). Cultural framing: Foreign correspondents and their work. *Education Resources Information Center*, 1–41.

Stark, R. W. (1962). Policy and the pros: An organizational analysis of a metropolitan newspaper. *Berkeley Journal of Sociology*, 11–31.

Sun, W. (2015). Configuring the foreign correspondent: New questions about china's public diplomacy. *Place Branding and Public Diplomacy*, *11*(2), 125–138. http://dx.doi.org/10.1057/pb.2014.20

Svensson, M., Sæther, E., & Zhang, Z. (2013). Agency, autonomy and voice among Chinese investigative journalists. In *Chinese Investigative Journalists' Dreams: Autonomy, Agency, and Voice*. Lexington, MA: Lexington Books.

Tai, Z. (2010). Casting the ubiquitous net of information control: Internet surveillance in China from golden shield to green dam. *International Journal of Advanced Pervasive and Ubiquitous Computing (IJAPUC)*, *2*(1), 53–70.

Tandoc, E. C., Jr. (2018). Five ways BuzzFeed is preserving (or transforming) the journalistic field. *Journalism*, *19*(2), 200–216.

Tong, J. (2011). *Investigative journalism in China: Journalism, power, and society*. New York and London: Continuum.

Tong, J. (2019). The taming of critical journalism in China: A combination of political, economic and technological forces. *Journalism Studies*, *20*(1), 79–96.

Townsend, J. (1992). Chinese nationalism. *The Australian Journal of Chinese Affairs*, (27), 97–130.

Tuchman, G. (1978). *Making news: A study in the construction of reality*. New York, N.Y.: The Free Press.

Tumber, H., & Prentoulis, M. (2005). Journalism and the making of a profession. *Making Journalists: Diverse Models, Global Issues*, *58*, 73.

Tunstall, J. (1974). *Journalists at work; specialist correspondents: Their news organizations, news sources, and competitor-colleagues* (Vol. 1). Thousand Oaks, CA: Sage Publications.

Underwood, D. (1988). When MBAs rule the newsroom. *Columbia Journalism Review*, *26*(6), 23.

Unger, J. (2016). *Chinese nationalism*. Abingdon, UK: Routledge.

Van Dalen, A. (2012). The people behind the political headlines: A comparison of political journalists in Denmark, Germany, the United Kingdom and Spain. *International Communication Gazette*, *74*(5), 464–483.

VanderKlippe, N. (2017, August 25). Detained in "the safest place" on Earth. *The Globe and Mail*, p. A16.

Van Ginneken, J. (1997). *Understanding global news: A critical introduction*. Thousand Oaks, CA: Sage Publications.

Vartanova, E. (2012). The Russian media model in the context of post-Soviet dynamics. In D. C. Hallin & P. Mancin (Eds.), *Comparing media systems beyond the Western world* (pp. 119–142). Cambridge: Cambridge University Press.

Voltmer, K. (2008). Comparing media systems in new democracies: East meets South meets West. *Central European Journal of Communication*, *1*(1), 23–40.

Voltmer, K. (2012). How far can media systems travel. In D. C. Hallin & P. Mancin (Eds.), *Comparing media systems beyond the Western world* (pp. 222–245). Cambridge: Cambridge University Press.

VonDoepp, P., & Young, D. J. (2012). Assaults on the fourth estate: Explaining media harassment in Africa. *The Journal of Politics*, *75*(1), 36–51.

Wacquant, L. (2014). Homins in extremis: What fighting scholars teach us about habitus. *Body & Society*, (2), 3–17.

140   *References*

Waisbord, S. (2002). Antipress violence and the crisis of the state. *Harvard International Journal of Press/Politics, 7*(3), 90–109.

Wakeman, C. (2001). Beyond the square. In *Covering China*. New Brunswick, NJ: Transaction Publishers.

Wang, J. (2017, May 7). (in Chinese). Misleading views of intent behind Belt and Road still common in Western media. *Global Times*. Retrieved from www.globaltimes.cn/content/1045739.shtml

Weaver, D. H., Beam, R. A., Brownlee, B. J., Voakes, P. S., & Wilhoit, G. C. (2007). *The American journalist in the 21st century: US news people at the dawn of a new millennium*. New York, NY: Routledge.

Weaver, D. H., & Wilhoit, G. C. (1996). *The American journalist in the 1990s: US news people at the end of an era*. Mahwah, NJ: Lawrence Erlbaum Associates.

White, D. M. (1950). The "gate keeper": A case study in the selection of news. *Journalism Bulletin, 27*(4), 383–390.

Wike, R., Poushter, J., Silver, L., & Bishop, C. (2017). Globally, more name US than China as world's leading economic power. *Pew Research Center, 13*.

Willnat, L., & Martin, J. (2012). Foreign correspondents: An endangered species? In *The global journalist in the 21st century* (pp. 495–510). New York, NY: Routledge.

Willnat, L., & Weaver, D. (2003). Through their eyes: The work of foreign correspondents in the United States. *Journalism, 4*(4), 403–422.

Wong, E. (2014, March 25). *Ex-Bloomberg editors tells why he left*. Retrieved from https://sinosphere.blogs.nytimes.com/2014/03/25/ex-bloomberg-editor-tells-why-he-left/

World Bank. (2018). *Belt and road initiative*. Retrieved from www.worldbank.org/en/topic/regional-integration/brief/belt-and-road-initiative

Wu, H. D., & Hamilton, J. M. (2004). US foreign correspondents changes and continuity at the turn of the century. *Gazette, 66*(6), 517–532.

Xinhua. (2014, July 5). *South Korean in Wangjing: How far is Beijing to Seoul?* Retrieved from www.xinhuanet.com/world/2014-07/05/c_1111473908.htm

Yemma, J. (2007). Instant connection: Foreign news comes in from the cold. In *From pigeons to news portals: Foreign reporting and the challenge of new technology* (pp. 47–69). Baton Rouge: Louisiana State University Press.

Young, A. (2013, March 18). Wall street journal didn't pay bribes in China, says publisher Dow Jones, as justice department investigates. *International Business Times*. Retrieved from www.ibtimes.com/wall-street-journal-didnt-pay-bribes-china-says-publisher-dow-jones-justice-1132449

Zelizer, B. (1993). Journalists as interpretive communities. *Critical Studies in Media Communication, 10*(3), 219–237.

Zelizer, B. (2004). *Taking journalism seriously: News and the academy*. London: Sage Publications.

Zhao, Y. (1998). *Media, market, and democracy in China: Between the party line and the bottom line* (Vol. 139). Urbana, IL: University of Illinois Press.

Zhao, Y. (2012). Understanding China's media system in a world historical context. *Comparing Media Systems Beyond the Western World*, 143–176.

Zeng, Y. (2018). Detached disseminator, populist watchdog and facilitative change agent: The professional role perception of foreign correspondents in China. *Journalism, 19*(9–10), 1397–1416.

Zeng, Y., & Song, Y. (2018). The social foreign correspondent: Reconfiguring journalistic branding research in the age of social media. *Popular Communication, 16*(4), 293–308.

Zheng, R. (2017, August 8). (in Chinese). *Why are Western media smearing China?* Retrieved from http://media.people.com.cn/n1/2017/0808/c40606-29455410.html

Zhu, J., & Lu, J. (2013). One rising China, multiple interpretations: China's 60th anniversary celebration through the lens of the world's printed media. *Journal of Contemporary China, 22*(84), 1067–1088.

Index

Note: Page numbers in *italics* indicate a figure and page numbers in **bold** indicate a table on the corresponding page.